Advar

A World in a Grain of Sand

Time and time again, Carol Van Klompenburg captivates readers with her unique vision of the world. She can draw you into the smallest detail, this time bringing life and perspective to often discarded items. In her latest tales, she travels short distances throughout her home and tells the stories of the items that she built her life around.

Carol transforms what may be viewed as just everyday household items, taking readers on a trip to places of yesteryear. Carol doesn't miss details, and her stories often make me wonder what the things I surround myself with will tell about my life someday.
Sarah Weber, Editor, *Sioux County Capital-Democrat*

A World in a Grain of Sand is stirring, lovely, and delightful. As I sat at my kitchen table reading it, Carol's stories and photographs made me look around and consider the artifacts in my own life.

Her stories and images transported me back into the lives of my own parents and grandparents. As I looked around, I saw remnants from their lives, now sprinkled in mine—their china, furniture, paintings, and books—and in the garage, all of my dad's tools.

Now I wonder which of their belongings and my own will survive into my children's and grandchildren's lives and perhaps even further generations.

Inspired, I am now considering which of these artifacts have stories I can share.
Dr. Robert Leonard is an anthropologist with bylines in the *New York Times*, *TIME*, *USA Today*, the *Des Moines Register*, the *Iowa Capital Dispatch*, and other publications. He lives in rural Marion County, Iowa.

My mother's tears as she sorted belongings for yet another move belied her words, "It's just stuff." Carol's stories prompted this memory along with the realization that Mom's tears were not for the "stuff," but the memories attached to them. This book is an invitation to look around and share the stories our "stuff" contains.
Kathleen Evenhouse, Author of *Less Than a Widow*

Perhaps we work too hard searching for beauty and meaning in renowned galleries. Carol Van Klompenburg points us in another, simpler and far more accessible direction. That beauty and meaning is as near as our fingertips—in the everyday objects surrounding us. It's in a grandmother's crocheted purse, or a bird house on the patio. In these simple, everyday objects, Carol hears a story, and teaches us how to hear one, too.

Maureen Rank, Author of *Unbalanced: Forsaking Balance for Budapest*

Carol Van Klompenburg's latest book *A World in a Grain of Sand: Lively Little Stories of Household Stuff* transforms the background of those ordinary objects now sitting in our homes and weaves them into wonderful anecdotes about everything from heirlooms and family memories to wooden shoes to cross cultural moments and beyond. Divided topically into eight sections, the reader will find the book is relatable, fun and easy to read, and sure to bring back some memories of their own.

Ann Visser, Retired journalism adviser, freelance journalist

Reading Carol's columns and short essays, I always enjoy her ability to find a fascinating topic where others might simply turn away without seeing something of interest.

Helen Boertje, age 91, Author of *When One Room Fits All,* former columnist in multiple publications. Her writing currently appears frequently on Facebook

A World in a Grain of Sand
Lively Little Stories of Household Stuff

Carol Van Klompenburg

Copyright © 2024 Carol Van Klompenburg

All rights reserved.

ISBN: 9798336987140

Dedication

To those who create beauty around the globe
and
To those who pass on stories to coming generations

Acknowledgments

I am grateful to:

Those who went before me and preserved and passed on their household treasures and their stories,

Readers who responded to my columns with encouragement and their own stories,

My long-term writing group members, Bob Hutzell and Anne Petrie, for their suggestions and thoughts in response to early drafts,

Doug Calsbeek, Sarah Weber, and Kyle Ocker, the newspaper editors who first saw the potential in lively little stories of household stuff,

Kate Hoksbergen, for transforming my thoughts about cover design into a work of art,

Anne Petrie, freelance copyeditor, who converted my text from newspaper style to book style and suggested other improvements along the way (any remaining errors are mine),

And my husband Marlo, who remains my first reader as I work and play with words and stories.

Contents

Preface 1

Section A: Heirlooms and Family Memories 5
   1 Ancestor Collages 6
   2 Family Legends 9
   3 Boomerang Gifts 11
   4 Grandma's Cookie Kettle 13
   5 Rescuing a Milk Can 16
   6 Dusting Henry 19
   7 Carving Collection 22

Section B: Changes 25
   8 What I Didn't Know 26
   9 For All, a Season 28
   10 Sometimes Plan B 30
   11 Rethinking My Crosses 32
   12 Flawed Embroidery 35
   13 Jewelry Table Nostalgia 38
   14 A Tale of Two Totems 41

Section C : Cross-Cultural Moments 45
   15 Delft Ring 46
   16 Guatemala Jewelry 49
   17 Mended Wings 52
   18 Left Behind 55
   19 Valuable Turquoise 58

Section D: Dramatic Moments, Personal and Historical 61

   20 Dolphins of Hope 62

   21 Lindbergh Bowl 65

   22 The Gift of Words.. 68

   23 Flute Player's Song... 71

   24 The Memorial Stone and the Cross.. 74

Section E: In Memoriam... 77

   25 Remembering Joan... 78

   26 The Eagle and the Clematis 81

   27 Sunday Purse 84

   28 Aunt Gert's Afghans.. 87

   29 Aunt Kathryn's Blanket 90

   30 Stillbirth Weaving 93

   31 Serenity Prayer 96

Section F: Epiphany Moments 99

   32 Butterfly Visit 100

   33 Friendship Carving 102

   34 The Last Supper 105

   35 Be Still and Know.. 107

   36 Guardian Angel 110

   37 Scarlet Ribbon 113

Section G: On the Lighter Side 117

   38 My Father's Brass... 118

   39 Mouse Phobia 120

   40 Bargain Clock.. 123

41 Wren House 126

  42 Puzzling Tale 129

  43 Three Scenes with a Mobile 131

  44 Chili Contest 134

Section H: Artists and Artisans 137

  45 How Deep Our Need 138

  46 Ceramic Pair 141

  47 Enjoying Monet 144

  48 Daughter of the Trees 146

  49 Missing Sheryl 149

  50 Scarred Piano 152

  51 Praying Hands 155

  52 Mysterious Processes 158

  Group Presentations Available 163

  Audience Praise for Carol's Presentations 164

  Other Recent Books by Carol Van Klompenburg 166

Preface

"It is only stuff," people sometimes say when they comfort themselves following a house fire or a smashed knickknack. But that statement is not totally true. Treasures have tales. They spark memories and stories.

My possessions are grains of sand in which I see a wider world. The wall hangings, pictures, pottery, surrounding me at home provide pleasure. I enjoy their beauty. Sometimes, confronted by news of poverty, I feel guilty about that pleasure.

My household belongings evoke memories of events, experiences, and friendships. They remind me of the past and of how my world has both changed and remained the same.

These days, I own less stuff. In 2020 my husband Marlo and I downsized and parted with one-third of our possessions. We selected furniture by asking what would appropriately fit into our smaller space. We decided on smaller items using the question: Does it spark joy?

After we settled in, as I enjoyed my new surroundings, I reflected on our past and present lives. I also thought of the future, even the future after I depart this earth.

Will my sons and their wives want our belongings? Probably not.

Will they feel guilty disposing of our possessions? Probably. At least a little.

I remember sorting my mother's treasure trove after her death: every card or letter she had ever received and carbon copies of many letters she wrote. *We cannot possibly keep all these,* I thought. I remember choosing from my parents' knickknacks, wondering *Why did they save this? What did it mean to them?*

When my siblings and I hoisted several loads of paper into a recycling bin and carried unwanted bric-a-brac onto a truck bound for a local thrift store, I felt sad—and a little guilty. *I wish I knew the history of this stuff.*

One day in 2023, as I sat at the dining room table, a new thought excited me. *I can write the anecdotes of my belongings for my children and grandchildren! And I can take pictures. Perhaps the stories will help them make informed decisions. Even if they choose to discard items, they will still have the photos and the tales.*

I walked through my home and garden and made a list of items with potential stories. Then I started writing them, one at a time. More items joined my list. I tested the pieces on members of my longstanding Pella Writing Group. To my surprise, they loved those tales and thought other readers would also be intrigued.

To test my group's opinion. I sent samples to several newspaper editors, proposing a weekly column, *It Has a Story.* The editors said yes! The columns began appearing each week in newspapers in Orange City, Oskaloosa, and Ottumwa, Iowa.

As the columns appeared, reader responses amazed me. One reader emailed me to provide her opinion about what an antique figurine might have originally held in its empty hands. Another thanked me for providing hope for parents of stillborn children. One couple wrote me their differing napping habits matched my husband's and mine. When a newspaper failed to run the accompanying photo for an African soapstone carving, a reader emailed to ask me to send her a digital photo of it. My grandmother's frugality impressed someone else. The reader observed that raising eleven children during the Great Depression was no easy task.

I also used columns for group presentations. When I performed selected columns for clubs and church groups, audience members told me they turned first to my column when they opened their weekly paper.

The complete stillness in a crowd after I finished a poignant tale told me the listeners' hearts had been touched. So did the tears in my brother's eyes during a family reunion, when he read the story of our grandmother's purse.

Many responders requested I keep writing. I did.

By mid-2024, I had written fifty-two little stories about my household stuff, enough for a year of columns and for a book. For newspaper publication, columns appeared just as I wrote them — in random order. For book publication, they are organized under topic headings, although many could fit several categories.

When I finished column fifty-two, I realized writing them had given me a gift. I appreciated my belongings even more than before starting to write. "It's just stuff" has become less true for me. After all, I mean the words I sing at Sunday morning worship: "This is my Father's world." His world includes the work of artists and artisans along with the world of human bonds and behaviors.

As the eighteenth-century poet William Blake wrote in the first two lines of *Auguries of Innocence*, as I wrote I began

> To see a World in a Grain of Sand
> And a Heaven in a Wild Flower

In providing this collection as a book, I hope:

- *A World in a Grain of Sand* becomes one of the beloved belongings of my descendants;
- the anecdotes help all readers see the larger world in their own grain-of-sand possessions and appreciate them even more;
- and readers will share some of their own lively little stories with their children and grandchildren.

With hope,
Carol Van Klompenburg
Fall 2024

Section A:
Heirlooms and Family Memories

1 Ancestor Collages

Twenty years ago, I created a pair of ancestor photo collections. My husband Marlo matted and framed them, and they now hang in our entry hall. One collage (above, on the left) houses Marlo's ancestors; the other displays mine. Each collection begins with our great-grandparents at the top, our grandparents in the middle section, and our parents at the bottom—three generations from each side of our family.

About my great-grandparents we know very little. They are shadowy figures with just a few enduring legends apiece. My maternal great-grandmother Hurmana Kiel died in childbirth, and her newborn daughter was raised by an aunt. Great-Grandpa Kiel continued to live at his home with his other children. When his son John married my grandmother, Great-Grandpa Kiel moved in with them.

One legend says his two youngest children also moved in with my grandparents. The other version says he moved in by himself. The family story, however, is very clear on this: he was a difficult man to live with. My Grandma Kiel said he was her schooling in patience. He was quick to anger, and he was dirty. He frequently tracked mud and manure onto my grandmother's clean floors.

My maternal Huisman great-grandparents lived into their nineties, and I have faint memories of them as looking ancient and speaking

Dutch. Early in their marriage Great-Grandpa Huisman had a falling out with the church, and from then on Great-Grandma Huisman attended worship services without him, taking her children with her. She eventually birthed and transported all eleven of them to Sunday worship.

Marlo, the youngest child of three, never met any of his great-grandparents. However, his cousin Roger Van Klompenburg researched the family tree and discovered Great-Grandma Greitje Van Klompenburg was widowed in the Netherlands. She immigrated to the United States with her four young children, then married USA widower Jacob Sinnema, the father of five. Eventually two of Greitje's daughters married two of Jacob's sons. We do not know if those step-sibling marriages created small scandals.

The only great-grandparent we know much about is E.J.G. Bloemendaal, Marlo's maternal great-grandfather who emigrated from the Netherlands to Iowa. He wrote *My America,* a book about his experiences, for people considering emigration. The book was originally written in Dutch and published in the Netherlands in 1911. Around 1965, his descendant Arnold Vander Wilt wanted an English version and asked northwest Iowa pastor Conrad Veenstra to translate it. Marlo inherited a dog-eared photocopy of that translation. In 2009 my company, The Write Place, republished that photocopy as a paperback book. *My America* provides us a detailed picture of E.J.G. Bloemendaal's life, values, and decisions as a Midwestern pioneer farmer. Marlo and I enjoy access to this insight into both his life and its broader picture of life as a pioneer in the Midwest.

We enjoy our ancestor photo collections, but we are sad we know little or nothing about our other great-grandparents. Our photo collections remind us that we are part of the flow of history. We have both ancestors and descendants. We see similarities in the faces of our great-grandparents, ourselves, and even our grandchildren.

The photo collections have motivated us to leave more complete records for future generations. In 2021, I wrote and published *Child of the Plains*, a paperback memoir about my childhood growing up in Orange City, Iowa. In 2022, Marlo completed *Looking Back*, a hardcover book with color photos. It included his ancestry, his childhood, and his adult life.

E.J.G. Bloemendaal didn't intentionally leave a written legacy. He wrote for his Netherlands contemporaries, encouraging them to emigrate. But it turned into a legacy for his descendants. Marlo and I have chosen the path that came accidentally to him—to leave a written legacy. We want to leave a few traces that we walked this earth. We loved and laughed and cried, and tried to contribute in some small way to the world's shalom.

When we pass on the photo collections, perhaps they will motivate our children to value and pass on their legacies as well.

2 Family Legends

My friend Mary treasures a slightly worn plate with an ornate alphabet inscribed on the rim, a plate she at first rejected. When her husband's parents, Bill and Bea, were decluttering, they gathered items they no longer wanted and asked their descendants to choose what they would like. When the choosing ended, Bill said sadly, "No one chose this plate. It was Harold's baby plate." Harold was his brother who had died from polio at age five.

"Oh!" said Mary. "I didn't know. Of course, I want Uncle Harold's plate."

She has displayed it in her living room ever since. Its story created its value.

Two crocheted white doilies perch atop pillows on my guest bed. Two orange carnival glass bowls sit on a shelf in my dining room. They have stories too. One doily and one bowl are from Grandma Kiel, the other two from Grandma Addink.

Grandma Addink's fingers, gnarled and knobby from rheumatoid arthritis, crocheted at the speed of light. In group gatherings, she compensated for her hearing loss by crocheting. She heard little of conversations. The less she heard, the more her fingers flew.

Grandma Kiel crocheted at a more relaxed pace, pausing from time to time to weigh in on the topic at hand.

Although they did Victorian-style handwork, neither grandmother was a dainty Victorian lady. They were Midwestern farm wives. Both of them helped butcher chickens, pigs, and steers, and they canned the meat. They preserved fruit from the orchard and vegetables from the garden. Crocheting was a way to bring low-cost beauty into a hardscrabble life.

Carnival glass brought beauty too. Known as the poor man's Tiffany, it was first created by Fenton Art Glass Company in 1908 as a way to bring beauty to lower-income homes. Glass was pressed into intricate scallops and cutouts. During manufacturing pieces were coated with a metallic salt, resulting in their trademark rainbow iridescence.

Fenton first tried to market the glassware at premium prices. That failed, so the company discounted it to carnival owners to give away as prizes, hoping to raise its visibility and popularity. That plan succeeded, and the product earned the nickname "carnival glass."

Both of my grandmothers' pieces are in the most popular color for carnival glass—a yellow-orange known as marigold. Since they are in the most common color and have no trademark embedded in their bases, their antique value is minimal.

I doubt that my thrifty grandmothers would have purchased these pieces. Grandma Addink married in 1910 and Grandma Kiel in 1914, so the timing would have been right for the bowls to be wedding gifts. I think it is more likely, though, that these bowls arrived later, perhaps as prizes brought home by sons whose accurate throwing skills won them at Midwest fairs or carnivals.

Grandma Kiel kept her carnival glass bowl, the smaller and lacier one, on a bedroom dresser for combs and hairpins. Grandma Addink kept hers in the curved-glass curio cabinet in her dining room.

Having gathered and written these bits of information, I have perhaps told more than I know. Already today, I am more sure of the details than I was yesterday when I was straining to recall them. And legends embroider facts.

In the coming days, when my children and grandchildren visit and I want them to have a sense of their heritage, I shall tell them the legend of the doilies and the carnival glass. And on that day, I shall be even more sure of its truth than I am today.

With each telling, our family legends gain credibility and power.

3 Boomerang Gifts

Two ceramic baking dishes perch on the glass-and-metal shelving in the corner near an oak table in our dining area. A brown bunny sits atop one dish, a pair of pumpkins atop the other. Hidden in a nearby cupboard drawer are a pair of mahogany plaques, a Delft Blue tile embedded in each. We purchased the casserole dishes; Marlo made the plaques.

What do they have in common? About four decades ago we carefully selected them as Christmas gifts for our parents. Both sets of parents lived in Orange City, Iowa.

We selected the baking dishes from the ceramics at Pella's Sunflower Pottery, owned by Bob and Connie Andersen. In contrast to most Pella residents, Bob and Connie fit the flower children stereotype, Bob with his salt-and-pepper beard and wire rims, Connie with her peasant dresses and long, frizzy-curly hair. (After four decades, however, I am no longer sure if her dresses and the hairstyle are facts or figments of my imagination.) Bob had earned a BFA from the University of Northern Iowa and was the potter; Connie helped with design and managed the business. They created a range of pottery, and we chose from the Regional Collection, rather than the more funky Organic Collection. The Regional Collection was definitely Midwestern, with its animal and farm themes, and was especially suited to our parents' Iowa kitchens. We thought the dishes would bring a bit of beauty and pleasure to their dining rituals.

We assured our parents that the pottery was oven and dishwasher safe, but neither mother ever used her dish for baking or serving food.

My mother placed it on a lace runner atop her dining room table, and later flanked it with the two Sunflower Pottery mugs we gave her. Marlo's mother set her dish in an honored place on her kitchen counter, and there it stayed.

To make the plaques, Marlo cut sixteen-inch wooden squares from a chunk of mahogany, drilled hanging holes, and then routed and varnished the wood. He inlaid antique Delft tiles he had bought at a Belgian flea market. The plaques were designed to decorate walls, and these did achieve their intended use in both of our parents' homes.

In the decades that followed, the Andersens moved from Pella to Connie's Iowa hometown, Kalona. They added other product lines, but the Regional Collection remained their most popular. We raised three sons and became empty nesters. Our parents aged and then died. The baking dishes and plaques became boomerang gifts: they returned to whence they had come.

After boomeranging, neither the pottery or the tiles are used in their intended fashion. The pottery, we now agree with our mothers, is too beautiful to use, so it is home decor on our glass-and-metal shelving.

The work of a professional potter has endured better than that of an amateur carpenter. The Delft sprang cracks over the years—perhaps from age or perhaps from pressure from wood shrinkage. We now use the Delft plaques as trivets—protecting our tables from hot pans and casserole dishes.

I like to think that when both items graced our parents' homes, our mothers and fathers glanced at them from time to time and thought fondly of us. I know that now the pottery and Delft have been returned to us, we do the same.

4 Grandma's Cookie Kettle

The ceramic cookie kettle that first belonged to my grandmother has a cracked lid, carefully glued so that the mending barely shows. I don't know who mended it—not my grandfather because he was no longer living when that cookie kettle arrived at my grandmother's house.

It was a Christmas gift from my parents after she was widowed. A family photo shows her sitting on our floral couch, the black cookie kettle on her lap, the box and wrapping paper next to her. She had joined us for our family's annual exchange of gifts.

To the best of my memory, she accepted the gift graciously, but I have no memory of her using it. Her traditional thin-as-wafers sugar cookies always came from much larger two-gallon glass jars. Having raised eleven children, she did not know how to make small batches of anything, and with fifty-one grandchildren, she still needed an ample supply.

I don't think she used the kettle, but she didn't dispose of it either, not even after the lid had cracked. I know this because my mother inherited the cookie kettle after grandma had died.

Grandma believed in saving everything, including wooden cheese boxes and rubber bands, and she reused aluminum foil. Although her cookware was old, stained, and dented, she did not believe in new pans. When her children pooled their money and bought her a new set of pots and pans, she refused the gift and made them return it. Her old set was good enough. It still worked, and she would not let her children waste good money on a new set. One of my aunts told me that story with chagrin in her voice. Secretly I smiled, admiring grandma's frugality. Grandma must have softened over the decades because she accepted a cookie kettle which she probably knew she would not use.

For my mother, the family frugality was revealed in her table service. Seeing the bent handles and the scratched surfaces of her table service, my siblings and I pooled our money and bought her a new set of tableware. She didn't ask us to return it. However, she put it on a hard-to-reach shelf and continued to use the old tableware, saving the new set for special occasions—which never came.

My kitchen frugality displays itself in the sherbet dishes from the 1950s, inherited from my parents. It's an unmatched collection of three different designs, which I suspect my parents found on one of the Orange City garage sales they frequented. Several of the dishes have chips out of their rims. Before using them, I inspect them for further chips and fragments of glass, wincing slightly as I picture a fragment of glass making its way into my mouth and either chipping a tooth or cutting the lining of my stomach or intestines. I suppress the thought, inspect the dishes, and use them anyway

When my husband and I downsized a few years ago, the people from whom we bought the house emailed us photos of a set of Pfaltzgraff dishes they no longer wanted. Would we be interested in the dishes if they simply left the set in the house? I responded with a resounding yes. I could upgrade my faded Corelle dishes and be frugal too. A double win.

When we moved, I disposed of my faded Corelle dishes, but kept the sherbet dishes. The Pfaltzgraff set had nothing similar.

Looking at my grandmother's cookie kettle and thinking of how she softened over the years, I think again of those chipped sherbet dishes which I use with trepidation. Perhaps I shall dispose of them and use the Pfaltzgraff bowls instead.

On second thought, I shall keep the intact ones and dispose only of those with the dangerous chips.

5 Rescuing a Milk Can

On the floor in our den, next to the television, stands a five-gallon metal milk can. Marlo bought it as a memento of his childhood on his father's farm sale about fifty years ago. The milk can reminded me of my childhood on the farm as well.

It stood in our garage for a few months. Then I removed the lid, set a pot of Swedish ivy in the top, and moved it to our living room. A few years later, I put the lid back on and painted it with a simple antique look, a fad at the time.

When there was no space for it indoors, I moved it to our open front porch where it rusted in the rain and humidity. Marlo's mother winced at the crusty patches. I had become oblivious to its deterioration, but she liked things to look just right.

Then she thought of a solution. "Would you mind," she asked hesitantly, "if I took it back with me to Orange City and asked Joyce to paint it?"

We didn't mind at all. In fact we liked the idea. Joyce Bloemendaal was a long-term acquaintance married to Marlo's cousin, and we had seen samples of her beautiful Hindeloopen-style painting. Another Dutch-themed item in our home would be just fine.

Marlo's mother returned the milk can to us, transformed. Its rust had disappeared and Joyce had beautified it with Hindeloopen. We set it in our new sunroom, which had replaced the open porch.

Hindeloopen is a folk-style painting style, first created by Dutch sailors living in the village of Hindeloopen in the early 1600s. The painting, typically blues, greens, and reds, provided an alternative income when work on the seas dwindled. The sailors imitated the Rosemaling folk painting they had seen on their voyages to Norway, complete with scrolling leaves and dainty flowers.

I had learned about Hindeloopen when I interviewed Sallie De Reus, a Norwegian transplant to Pella who did both Rosemaling and Hindeloopen painting. I admired Sallie's work, but interviewing her did not result in my immediate purchase of Hindeloopen. It did, however, result in a gazebo studio.

When I had met with Sallie, she took me to see her studio—a tiny shed on the yard of the De Reus farm. She regularly left her house to paint there. I didn't envy Sallie's artistic talent because I did not aspire to be a painter. But I did envy her studio. How wonderful it would be to escape to a studio when I wanted to write!

I mentioned my envy of Sallie's studio to my husband Marlo. Later, when we replaced our warped front door and our sliding glass doors for energy efficiency, Marlo remembered my comment. He could reuse the five sliding glass doors as giant windows along with the warped front door for a gazebo. A friend offered us two more used patio doors. Marlo could now create an eight-sided gazebo in our backyard. It would work as a greenhouse in the spring, and for the rest of the year it could be my studio.

Months later, Marlo completed the gazebo and vowed never to build a structure that complicated again. I reveled in a studio where I could escape to write. We hung a hammock in it and put in a desk and chair. On warm days, I opened the windows and enjoyed the breeze. On sunny winter days, the passive solar heat from the cement floor brought the temperature in the gazebo up to seventy degrees.

When I carried my laptop into the gazebo, an instant studio surrounded me. I could look out all seven windows and the windowed door panel and write—using a notebook in the hammock or the laptop on the desk.

Marlo and I have downsized to a smaller home, so I no longer have the gazebo. The Pella library has become my getaway studio instead. The milk can, its Hindeloopen still pristine, sits in our den. It has become a many-windowed link to the past.

These days I see in it not only our childhoods on the farm, but also Sallie, Joyce, and my mother-in-law. All three women appreciated beauty, made space for it in their lives, and have inspired me to do the same.

6 Dusting Henry

When my father, Henry Addink, died in 2014 and my mother moved to an assisted-living apartment, my siblings and I divided what she could not keep. We took turns, each of us selecting an item in sequence.

A blue figurine with an orange cap called out to me. Dad had inherited it from my grandparents, and it had stood in my parents' curio cabinet for decades. After it had stood on our shelving for several years, I started thinking of it as Henry.

The six-inch-figurine's brimmed cap reminded me of a softball cap and Dad's pleasure playing that game.

He served mostly as a first baseman on our church team, but occasionally, when their customary pitcher Paul ran out of pitching steam, Paul insisted on playing first base and Dad moved to center field.

My clearest memory of Dad's play is in this position. I was thirteen, and he was thirty-six. Sitting in the bleachers, I was already embarrassed because I thought him much too old to be playing softball. He had been balding at twenty-five, and now his pate gleamed under the ball field lights.

A heckler from a seat near me yelled, "Put out that light in center field!" The crowd guffawed. I wanted to crawl under the bleachers.

The moment passed, and ten years later, I felt proud Dad still played. In his fifties, he switched to umpiring, and when he called balls and strikes, his voice rang out as loud as that heckler's had. Dad's energetic aging has served as a role model for me.

Today, as I dust, I study Henry, and for the first time I notice a smooth hole in his right hand. The hole is not from damage. It is a molded part of his hand and too small to hold a bat.

What did it hold? I wonder. Perhaps a fishing pole?

I think of Grandma Addink and her love of fishing for bullheads in Northwest Iowa rivers. I picture her on her fishing stool with her line in the water. She enjoys the breeze and waits for a bite. She can't see the bullheads, but she knows they are out there in the muddy water.

I enjoyed fishing in childhood and adolescence. I no longer fish, but I think my freelance writing is a form of fishing with words. Will editors or readers grab the word bait I cast onto the waters of the publishing world? Will readers email responses? I don't know, but, like Grandma, I love casting the line.

I stop dusting, and I photograph Henry. I paste the photo of this softball-or-fisher boy into Google Images. About thirty almost identical images pop up with accompanying information. They are for sale.

I learn that Henry is bisque—unglazed china. He was hand painted after kiln firing. I read he was made in Japan. I check under his feet and on his back, where it says in both places, "Made in Japan." I haven't ever noticed this before.

Some entries call him a "frozen Charlie doll" because his arms and legs are immovably molded as part of him.

I am surprised to read his brimmed cap, a circle made of pie-piece sections, was worn by newsboys, not ball players. I sigh.

Then the information gets messy. Some owners say he dates back to the 1920s; others claim he originated in the 1950s. Some owners say he is the comic strip character Smitty from *Gasoline Alley*.

In the Wikipedia listing for "Gasoline Alley," however, there is no character named Smitty. When I look at samples of the comic, I find Smitty, but he doesn't look at all like my Henry.

I wonder about that hole in Henry's hand. One owner says it probably held flowers. In one photo, though, Henry holds a remnant of string. That owner says it is the remains of a leash, but the attached puppy has been lost. Another owner confirms the puppy and leash story. I sigh again. There goes my fishing pole story.

The information I have found is contradictory. The information may be based on an owner's desire to sell an antique. I am not convinced about his comic strip character origins. But I am convinced the figurine stories I created about softball and fishing are figments of my imagination.

I created myth for Henry, not history. But the memories evoked by those myths still have power. I know that whenever I dust him, he will bring to mind my father and my grandmother along with the traits they have modeled and passed on.

7 Carving Collection

"What can we get Dad for Christmas? For Father's Day? For his birthday?" It was a question our sons often asked me when they were growing up.

And for many years, their first choice, instead of a tie or a handkerchief, was a hand-carved wooden animal. We went to the downtown Pella store together. They counted up their savings, and they selected a carving they could afford.

Gradually a collection of carvings grew. It now sits atop the bookshelves in our great room.

The collection includes a lion, a hippo, two cats, two antelope, four elephants, and five giraffes. The lion is primitive, its mane crudely carved. Many others show great skill.

Some are especially appealing. A baby giraffe nurses while his mother towers above him, her long neck curved down so she can nudge him with her nose. A cat peers down, her nose draped over the edge of the shelf. Another sleeps, her body curled in a circle. A baby elephant is in the womb of its mother, both carved from a single piece of wood.

Each year we shopped for the carvings in the same Pella store, The Work of Our Hands. It is a fair-trade store that was launched in Pella in 1990. Each carving was handmade by an artisan from a developing country, such as Indonesia, Thailand, Kenya. The items were made and purchased under Fairtrade International standards.

The goal of Fairtrade International standards is "to tackle poverty and empower producers in the poorest countries in the world." Small-scale producers and workers are among the most marginalized by the global trade system. In the Fairtrade system, producers must receive a price which covers the average cost of production. No forced labor or child labor is permitted. Food producers and artisans have a fifty percent vote in the organizations handling their merchandise. Each Fairtrade organization is independently certified as adhering to these standards and more.

Eventually, to our disappointment, The Work of Our Hands discontinued the carved animals. The store still carried fair-trade items, but either those carvings had saturated the local market or public taste shifted to other products.

Our sons became adults, and sometimes when they asked for my Christmas wish list, I simply said, "Anything from a fair-trade store." And when I opened my gift of handmade jewelry or home decor, I pictured the men and women in their homes or small shops plying their craft, receiving fair wages, and finding a path out of poverty.

Buying a fair-trade item creates a double gift: a beautiful handmade item for a recipient and a living wage for an artisan in a developing country.

After downsizing, our space for new home decor has shrunk. But I still enjoy buying fair-trade consumables, such as coffee, chocolate, and olive oil.

When I sit at the table cradling a cup of coffee at breakfast, the mug warms my hands.

And when I look toward the carving collection, the memories warm my heart.

Section B: Changes

8 What I Didn't Know

Except for paint-by-number crafting, the only painting I have ever created hangs on my garage wall. A jade figurine in a hat sits behind yellow flowers spilling from a wicker basket. I painted it in a community-education class in 1975, the first year of my marriage.

Like me, the instructor was in his twenties. Although he was passionate about painting, he barely tolerated our community education class. He would have preferred teaching graduate students who already had degrees in visual arts, but he was stuck with us wannabes and our rudimentary painting skills.

It has been forty-eight years since I painted the flowers and figurine. I don't remember what our instructor looked like. I don't remember whether we practiced mixing paints before attempting to create on canvas. I don't remember what my husband Marlo painted as he took the class along with me.

I do remember this: I didn't know what to paint at first. But I found an old painting from my mother's attic, inherited from her mother. I set out to copy it. I enjoyed the process—dipping my brush in the colors, then blending and shaping the flowers, basket, and figurine. I first worked on it at home, and I had painted more than half of it before the teacher told me I had chosen to copy a painting with very poor composition. I hadn't realized its poor structure. After all, it had a frame and had been sold commercially in decades past.

Neither did I realize that the figurine in the Japanese hat sat in the yoga lotus position. I didn't know I would later take yoga and sit in this position myself. In East Asian cultures, the sacred lotus symbolizes growth toward perfection and enlightenment, its roots in mud and its blossoms lifted toward the sun.

I didn't realize that the figurine's hands were raised higher than the typical lotus position in which arms rest on knees. Were his arms perhaps raised in blessing? That's what I imagine now. I didn't know his hat was called Kasa in Japan and could be a symbol of Buddhism worn by pilgrims and by monks in search of alms.

I didn't know I would become a gardener and grow those yellow flowers with dark centers, those black-eyed Susans native to Iowa. I didn't realize I would own a succession of houseplants in wicker baskets.

I didn't know that the original painting would disappear from my parents' attic, and my copy would be all that remained. I didn't know that the painting would hang in my office for years, and then when we downsized it would be relegated to the garage because our downsized house allowed no space for it.

Our past fades in the mists of memory. Our future is unknown. But we do receive the gift of moments we can enjoy with paint flowing from the tip of a brush as we dip and stroke and blend and shape.

As I did then with paint.

As I do now with words.

9 For All, a Season

Three wooden shoes sit on the shelves in our great room. Not one of them has a mate, and all are far too small for my size-eleven feet. All are painted with Hindeloopen—folk painting that originated in the tiny Dutch fishing village by the same name.

Wooden shoes are an appropriate decorative motif for my husband Marlo and me. The name Van Klompenburg means "from the wooden shoe town."

But why unmated shoes instead of pairs? Because they are trophies. In the 1990s, Pella Tennis Club sponsored tournaments. Because Pella (the town in which we live) treasured its Dutch heritage, that club awarded Hindeloopen-painted wooden shoes to the winners instead of gilded trophies.

I had enjoyed tennis as exercise for a decade. At age forty-four I invited Kathy, whose skills exceeded mine, to partner with me in playing some tournaments. That summer, instead of just once each week, I played tennis three times per week—and on tournament days that could be three to six matches. My game improved. My ground strokes sent balls in the direction I intended. However, I never could put much speed on the ball. Kathy and I won matches in B-level tournaments in other Iowa towns, too, winning medals or traditional trophies as awards.

After two summers dedicated to tennis, Kathy moved out of state, and I decided to invest less time in the sport. I had other interests, such as gardening and writing. I started a flower garden and launched The Write Place, a writing and graphic arts service.

Each summer I expanded my perennial beds. I added a few staff members to The Write Place and moved the business from my basement to downtown Pella.

Playing less tennis lowered my skill level. As my skills shrank, my pleasure in the game also declined. After each match I felt exhausted. My joints and muscles ached. "It's just not fun anymore," I told my husband Marlo as he headed for the courts alone. "Have a good time."

The trophies began in the living room, moved to my office, and—as the memories of the out-of-town tournaments faded—were eventually trashed. The wooden shoes remained.

As my perennials multiplied, I split them and started selling plants to fund garden expenses, which were becoming significant. In 2009, initial sales were a few hundred dollars; by 2019 they totaled a few thousand. I participated in local garden tours and wrote a book about gardening.

When I retired, I turned over Write Place management to a staff member who eventually bought the business. In retirement, Marlo and I took up pickleball—a sport that was growing popular with older people. We saw it as a sport for former tennis players. It required the same skill set but was easier on our bones and muscles. The ball was slower, the court was smaller, and the racket was lighter.

As I approached 70, the gardening became more difficult and less fun. I began hiring help with the mulching and weeding, using some of the funds from plant sales. Marlo grew weary of snow blowing, mowing, and transporting garden waste to the local landfill.

We downsized to a duplex which has only foundation plantings and a tiny flower garden next to the patio. We hired out the mowing and snow blowing.

I recently downgraded my pickleball game, and switched to playing in a lower-skill-level group, which had become a better match for me. Marlo continues to play in the higher-level group. I can feel the day approaching when perhaps I will also say of pickleball, "It's just not fun anymore."

Someday, the tennis memories may fade even further, and the wooden shoe trophies, too, may disappear. But then again, they might remain as reminders of the meaning of our name.

10 Sometimes Plan B

Twenty years ago, we received two gifts: a player piano that didn't play and a piano stool.

The piano was given to us by a couple who no longer wanted it. They knew Marlo had restored pianos in the past and asked if he would be interested in restoring a player piano. He said yes.

The piano stool was a gift from Marlo's mother who knew we would need a bench or stool to go with the piano, saw one in an antique store, and bought it for us. (At least that's how Marlo remembers it. I could have sworn we bought it for ourselves.)

The piano didn't cost money, but it did require lots of grunt work to move it from its basement location. Marlo removed its wheels so it would fit through the low-ceilinged stairway, attached our piano-moving rollers, and found three strong friends. They tugged, lifted, and pushed it from the basement to our waiting trailer and then from the trailer into Marlo's basement shop. To thank the team, he treated them to Breadeaux pizza.

Early the next morning the telephone woke us. It was the couple's neighbor and distant relative, convinced she had first rights to the piano. "They had no right to give it to you," she said.

An expert at dodging confrontation, Marlo took a deep breath, exhaled, and said gently, "If you feel you have a right to the piano, you may have it. But I have considerable labor invested in it. It took four of us several hours to move it. Plus I provided pizza for the movers. I think that is worth about $100. For $100, I will be willing to part with the piano."

Silence fell. "I'll think about it," she said. She never called back.

Marlo designated the piano as a retirement project, so it sat in his workroom for a couple of decades. The piano stool became a temporary lampstand in our guest bedroom—until it would be needed for the piano.

Retirement came. Marlo started to dismantle the piano innards and discovered that its player-piano parts were beyond repair. He had only been interested in it as a player piano. He already had a baby grand with a matching bench. How could we dispose of the player piano? Marlo removed the cover, the keys, the strings, and the huge metal plate that held the strings. I looked at the metal plate and saw potential as garden art. Marlo looked at the remaining piano frame and saw a potential workbench. We re-purposed them. We fastened the metal plate vertically in the garden under our backyard deck. Marlo adapted the piano frame as a workbench for his powered miter saw. The piano stool remained in the guest bedroom.

When we downsized, we parted with about a third of our possessions. We left the giant metal plate in the garden. We chopped up the miter saw table, but we kept the piano stool. It became a tiny table for our TV and DVD remotes.

Neither the piano nor the piano stool achieved its intended purpose. Sometimes in life, when Plan A is a dead end, Plan B works just fine.

11 Rethinking My Crosses

Several months ago, reading an online newsletter, I stumbled upon a critique of a woman wearing a diamond-studded, silver cross pendant while making a political announcement on television.

As I recall, that writer said it was a sacrilege to use the cross where Jesus suffered as a beautiful ornament.

I stopped reading and considered the crosses in my home: a wooden cross, a plaster cross, and a cross made from slices of walnut shells. All were beautiful. Should I remove them from my walls?

When I placed those crosses above two light switches and on a bathroom wall, I placed them where I would see them often and be reminded of Christ.

They were empty crosses, not crucifixes with Christ still suffering on them. My Protestant theology had taught me our crosses are empty to remind us that Christ is no longer on that cross. On the third day, he rose to life.

After reading the online article, I considered each of my crosses. It would be difficult to part with them. In addition to being reminded of Christ, I have a historical attachment to each of them.

I purchased the wooden cross on a Cambodia learning tour to view the work of World Renew, a non-profit agency of my religious denomination. That cross reminds me of the servant-hearted assistance to the least, the last, and the lost, lived out by World Renew's Cambodian staff. And carved into the cross are Khmer words meaning "always with us." I believe that Christ is always with me through his Spirit.

The walnut-shell cross was given to me decades ago by Marian, a next-door neighbor, who crafted beautiful decor by gluing together the ornate beauty of thinly sliced walnut shells. After I published a newspaper article about her hobby, she gifted me with a walnut cross. Humble, gentle, and generous, she has been a role model for me ever since.

The plaster cross called out to me in a US gift shop with a butterfly silhouette in its center inscribed with the Bible verse, "Be still and know that I am God" (Psalm 46:10). Those words have been a mantra for me most of my adult life.

I researched displaying crosses and discovered this use has a centuries-long history, both in churches and in homes. Online I found a few writers who thought crosses violated the second commandment, which forbids using images for worshiping God. But a majority of writers articulated the opposite opinion. I found the majority opinion more convincing.

I discovered no other writers objecting to beautiful crosses as sacrilegious or disrespectful of Christ's suffering. I hunted for that original critique and failed to find it.

Then I remembered that online newsletter critique had said wearing the cross pendant was shameful because the woman had used it for a political purpose: to spark buy-in for her message among Christian viewers. I did not hang my crosses to support a political message!

I decided to keep them.

However, the original article had brought to mind that the cross was a place of indescribable suffering. I resolved to keep Christ's suffering in mind when one of my crosses came into view.

I soon forgot that resolution.

The article faded in my memory as I went about the details of day-to-day living.

Then, one afternoon as I ended my volunteer shift at The Well (a local Christ-based, social service agency), my supervisor handed me a large wooden cross. An area woodworker had donated a box of them and instructed him they are not to be sold, but to be given away to Well volunteers. I accepted the cross, said thanks, and drove home.

Seated at the dining room table, I studied this new cross. It was bigger than my other crosses and far less beautiful. It featured unvarnished wood burned with dark stripes. Giant nails were embedded both vertically and horizontally.

"I don't like this cross. It is so rough-hewn," I told my husband Marlo. "But I don't feel right trashing it. Let's hang it in the garage next to our framed puzzles."

Marlo, who usually hangs our home decor, took the cross and said little.

After a couple of hours in his garage workshop, he reappeared with the cross and asked, "Could I show you something?"

He led me to our bedroom, placed the cross on an empty wall above his dresser, and ventured, "What do you think of this location?"

He paused and added, "I'm not sure it looks good next to those puzzles. It is so different from them . . ." His voice trailed off.

As I studied his suggested location, I saw again the nails and burnt wood. I recalled the online article insisting we remember the cross as a place of great suffering.

This cruder cross would contrast with the other three.

I changed my mind.

"Yes," I told Marlo. "Yes. Thank you. It will be good to have it there."

Perhaps now I would remember more often the shadow side of the cross: Christ's indescribable and immeasurable suffering.

12 Flawed Embroidery

Lifting a box of gift bags from a closet shelf, I uncover a rectangle of embroidered fabric. When framed in past years, it hung from a wall, a family room wall, I think. When we moved to this smaller home four years ago, I detached the frame and demoted the stitchery to a closet shelf.

A border, along with pearl-and-floss flowers, surrounds seven lines of words:

A World in a Grain of Sand

In
memory of
Craig Evan
Van Klompenburg
stillborn
on
Oct. 29, 1982

I pause. I remember back forty-two years.

The young doctor filling in for my normal physician removed his stethoscope from my huge abdomen and said, puzzled, "I can't hear a heartbeat. Let's do a Doppler ultrasound." The Doppler could hear no heartbeat either.

The nurse doing the Doppler called my husband. He rushed over. We drove to Des Moines for another ultrasound (a picture this time) and a specialist. The specialist gently told us, "All indications are the baby has died and that you are in labor. You will probably deliver in the next twenty-four hours."

We went home. We told our sons Chad and Mark their baby brother Craig had died within me.

Chad, age six, sat motionless in his chair and murmured, "I wish you hadn't told me that," as if not hearing the news would keep it from being true. Age three, Mark didn't understand what had happened. We sat in quiet for a few minutes.

Then I emptied the dishwasher, vacuumed carpet, and sorted clutter, frantic to distract myself with something I could control. I craved order in the chaos that suddenly engulfed my life and plans.

That night in the delivery room I heard no newborn's first cry, only the clank of delivery tools on a metal table.

My parents arrived the next day.

We held a private service at the funeral home, facing a tiny white casket draped with flowers.

In the days that followed, we mourned. Sometimes we wept. My husband cried as he took down the baby crib. I sobbed as I boxed the baby clothes. We wept together in bed through the long nights.

My parents stayed a week. My mother asked for household cleaning jobs.

A few weeks after they left, my mother sent us a package. I was reluctant to open it.

When I did, I discovered a hand-embroidered memorial to Craig. I was amazed. In the decades as her daughter, I had never before seen her do a single stitch of needlework. The border was beautiful and flawless. The hand-stitched lettering was legible, but uneven in places. I concluded she had purchased a kit which provided guidelines for the intricate border and flowers. But, of course, she had needed to stitch in the words without a guide.

I suspected the unevenness bothered her. Her handwriting was impeccable. It had been perfect on the letter she left on the dresser of the nursery when she and Dad had traveled home.

In her flawless handwriting, she had left me two pages of grieving instructions: "You need to cry more after Dad and I have left. You and Marlo must not let this loss drive you apart . . ."

I no longer remember the rest of her instructions in that letter. I read it, raged, and then grew more furious reading it the second time. I felt violated. I tore it up and threw it in the garbage.

Forgiving her was a long process.

You see, the letter followed decades of wounds as the daughter of a woman who lacked personal boundaries. She was incapable of recognizing where she ended and another person began. She experienced the lives of her children as if those lives were hers, even when we were adults.

Holding her handiwork, today, my anger with her shortcomings rises again for a moment.

Then I remember my own miscarried grandson, and recall the loss I felt. I picture my mother's similar loss. I imagine her struggling to complete this needlework amid tears.

I think also of her pleasure in learning new words before her eventual dementia and death. I remember her notebooks of proverbs, recorded each time she read a maxim she especially liked. I didn't learn about those notebooks until she thought they were lost. She had loaned them to a friend in a nursing home, and she was inconsolable after her friend misplaced them.

When her notebooks were found, I helped her convert them into a paperback book, *Treasury of Gems*, which she proudly sold or gave away to friends and relatives, sharing her viewpoints, this time in a non-invasive way.

Holding her flawed embroidery, I forgive her yet again for her letter of grief instructions. Peace returns.

I put her handiwork back on the shelf. Although I continue to downsize, I will not purge it. It has led me to forgive again. It no longer belongs on my walls, but I will not part with it today.

13 Jewelry Table Nostalgia

Last Christmas I considered giving my fifty-year-old jewelry table to my adolescent granddaughter Elise. But then my son told me someone had already purchased a jewelry box for her, and I abandoned the idea.

My French Provincial jewelry table was a Christmas gift from my parents in 1971, my first year of teaching. My college friend Carol Hoekman helped my mother choose it.

As Dordt College classmates, Carol and I both majored in English, intending to teach high school. We became close friends during the final semester of our senior year. We were both nerds who rarely dated, loved studying, and thought we would also love teaching. We didn't.

While student teaching we were shocked to discover running a classroom was totally different from being a student. Our first two weeks in the classroom exhausted us.

In addition, as graduation neared, our classmates announced engagements and displayed diamond rings with frightening frequency. Potential lifelong spinsterhood terrified us.

We became confidantes. We spent long evenings together in the campus coffee shop. We bemoaned the challenges of adolescent classrooms and our impending lifelong single state. We both made weekly visits to the college counselor's office, and we bonded as we compared notes on those visits.

Then we graduated. Carol taught in Orange City, Iowa, my hometown. Hungry for city life, I taught in Lansing, Illinois, a south Chicago suburb. Our friendship faded.

Looking at the jewelry table a few weeks ago, I remembered Carol and wondered, *Whatever became of Carol Hoekman? We were once so close. I would like to talk with her again.*

Since 1971, I had received just one letter from her, probably around 1979. Her letter said she moved to Colorado and married. She and her husband, Jean La Perriere, were launching a jewelry-making business.

After decades of silence, I suddenly hungered to reconnect with Carol. *Did their business survive? Are they still in Colorado?*

I searched the internet. I found no listing for Carol, but I found an email address for Jean La Perriere, La Perriere Manufacturing, Lake Placid, Florida. An email I sent came back undeliverable.

I searched for obituaries for both Jean and Carol and found none. But I found obituaries for some of Carol's siblings. One sister, Edith Hemmeke, apparently still lived. I located her on Facebook and messaged her. She messaged back within an hour.

Yes, she was Carol's sister. Carol had indeed moved from Colorado to Florida. Carol died from pancreatic cancer in 2019. Jean died three years later. I was shocked. I wanted to learn more about Carol's life. I messaged Edith again. She said she would be glad to tell me more via telephone, and she did.

Carol and Jean's jewelry business fizzled after a couple of years, and they used the jewelry-making equipment to manufacture small parts for the airline industry instead. That succeeded. With most of their customers in southeastern states, they moved their business to Florida.

Carol worked in the business and taught English from time to time to supplement their income. A skilled musician, she also played organ for a variety of churches, eventually becoming the organist for St. James Roman Catholic Church in Lake Placid, where she and Jean decided to worship.

I thanked Edith for being willing to talk with me, and our conversation ended. Over the next few hours I thought about Carol's life and mine.

Our lives had some parallels: Both of us left high school teaching after that first year. Then Carol found secretarial work in Colorado, and I became a college teaching assistant. Despite our fear of spinsterhood, in 1975 we both married. We had no daughters, only sons, and each had a son who struggled with addiction. Like Carol, I connected with Roman Catholicism. In recent decades I enjoyed books by Catholic mystics, and I began the Benedictine practice of Lectio Divina with a group of friends. I remained, however, a Protestant.

After talking with Edith, I knew more of Carol's story, but I still felt empty, sad, and nostalgic. *What am I seeking?* I wondered. I gradually realized that I ached to recreate sitting across that college coffee shop table from her. *I want to ask her questions, and learn about her inner journey over the years. I don't want information. I want our former relationship back.*

As I reflected, I studied the jewelry table. *Carol is gone. She is part of the past that can be remembered but not changed or retrieved.*

I turn toward the future. Last Christmas, the jewelry table wasn't appropriate for Elise, but in the future she might appreciate an antique jewelry table from her grandmother. *I can't change the past, but I can shape the future.*

I trudged to my office and pulled out my manila file labeled "For our executor."

Then I added a sentence to my other executor instructions. "I would like my jewelry table to go to my granddaughter Elise. Please tell her that in 1971, my first year of teaching, my parents gave it to me for Christmas."

14 A Tale of Two Totems

As she enters my front door, Marianne says, "I recognized your house when I saw the . . ." She hesitates, uncertain what to call the metal and glass pole next to my front door.

"The totem pole?" I supply the name my husband Marlo and I use for it. I tell Marianne that glass artist Sheryl Ellinwood called it a totem when she created a pair of them for us twenty or so years ago.

A World in a Grain of Sand

Marianne has arrived to pick up a copy of *Creative Aging*, a book I published in 2023.

Like most of Sheryl's art in and around my home, the totem pole was a bartered purchase in which Sheryl traded her artwork for my writing services. While she created it, she let me help choose the order for the red, blue, and yellow fused glass to be inserted into the empty shapes in the metal.

As we worked, she said she gave each pole a height and set of glass shapes slightly different from its mate's. She explained the asymmetry gave them more energy.

When completed, the totems flanked a tiny wooden bridge that spanned a dry creek bed in our entry garden. I had considered putting an arbor above that bridge, but when Sheryl suggested her totems as a barter option, I knew instantly they would flank the entry bridge.

To stabilize them in the landscaping, Marlo attached large squares of wood to their metal bases and drove spikes through the wood into the ground. We covered the wood bases with pink granite rock we were using as entry garden ground cover. During Iowa's erosive winters, we took the totems indoors. Sheryl had told us they were weather resistant, but we wanted to be sure they retained their dramatic colors.

In 2020 when we downsized, we discarded the wooden bases and moved the totems with us, along with our patio table and chairs. We arranged them all on our new backyard patio.

We set one totem at each corner of the patio. The totem's square metal bases, smaller than the wooden ones Marlo had previously added, appeared stable on the flat cement. We had found them a new home!

The move of the table was less satisfying. We discovered its center support had rusted dangerously over the years. Marlo removed the support and temporarily placed the tabletop directly on the cement. It would take effort, but perhaps he could build a new table base.

Then came a midnight windstorm that crashed both totems to the ground. The glass on one shattered; the glass on the other survived. We mourned the broken one and rejoiced in the survival of the other. However, a single totem was too small to look good on a spacious patio.

We chose a new location for it near the front door. Marlo created a new large wooden base, and anchored it by again driving spikes into the ground. We covered the base with gray landscaping stones.

We returned to the patio and studied the broken totem in somber silence. Sheryl had died five years earlier. The glass was irreplaceable. We studied some more. Then Marlo said, "Well... I suppose I could use the bottom half of the totem as a new table support."

I shrugged my shoulders and offered a slow nod.

Over the next few days, Marlo removed the detachable top half of the pole. He attached long wooden cross braces to the square metal base of the other half and mounted the cement tabletop on its opposite end. Voila! The patio table was restored.

To borrow from Charles Dickens, adjusting to the move "was the best of times, it was the worst of times."

And so it came to pass in the days of the Van Klompenburg retirement that one Sheryl Ellinwood totem welcomed Marianne at the front of our home and the other supported the table on the backyard patio.

Section C:
Cross-Cultural Moments

15 Delft Ring

On my finger as I keystroke today is an old ring. Its band is tarnished metal, inset with a half-inch circle of Delft. I bought it in 1971.

At twenty-three, I decided to tour Europe after a college had offered me a teaching assistantship in German. I accepted the job, but after a year of no German, I knew my skills were rusty.

After just one year of teaching high school on a $6,000 salary, I had some savings. I borrowed the popular tour guide, *Europe on $5 a Day*, from a friend. As the book advised, I would stay in youth hostels, travel on a one-month Eurail pass, and eat cheap. I decided I could afford the trip.

The same frugal part of me that had accumulated savings was thrilled that I would be able to list the plane flight and the expenses in Germany as a tax deduction.

Arthur Frommer had written *Europe on $5 a Day* in 1957. Concerned about inflation, I invested in an updated version. "Plan on $10-15 per day instead," it advised. Could I still afford a trip to Europe to tune up my language skills? Yes, but barely.

I would buy no souvenirs. I couldn't afford them. Besides, I wouldn't have room for mementos in my small suitcase. Backpacks, already popular among students, would make travel easier, but they cost money. My only souvenirs would be my photographs. When I returned, I could develop the film when my cash flow allowed.

Thinking about safety in numbers, I recruited former college classmates John and Joyce to join me. Using my travel guide, we planned a month's tour of Great Britain, France, the Netherlands, and, of course, Germany.

I wrote my parents that my summer arrival at their home would be delayed until July: "John, Joyce, and I will be traveling Europe in June!"

My mother knew I was a small-town girl whose only independent travel experience was one trip to New York City to see an older cousin. Mother was terrified. She told me so. "Are you sure about this trip? I won't sleep a wink."

I tried to allay her fears. Yes, I was sure. We were intelligent adults. We had a guidebook and the necessary funds. All of us had a year of teaching experience. We could handle anything.

I was right. In Europe we met only a few minor snags. A scruffy German persistently tried to join us on a walking tour. He wanted to convert our threesome into a pair of couples. We declined politely. Then less politely. He gave up.

On a night of hotel room shortages in Great Britain, Joyce and I were forced to share our room with John. We remained celibate. To avoid scandal, we vowed not to report the event to our families. Neither would we report that some youth hostels provided only one huge dorm room, shared by both men and women.

In the Netherlands, we crossed a canal in a car borrowed from Dutch friends. Then we turned right at the corner immediately after the canal, as the locals near that canal had instructed us. The road narrowed. Then narrowed more. If we continued, the car, loaned to us by Dutch friends, would plunge into the canal. We reversed and inched back to the turnoff where our local advisers had collapsed over a railing, guffawing at the Americans' inability to distinguish a sidewalk from a street.

Making the correct turn, we found the city square we were seeking. We browsed among the trinket vendors. I planned to buy nothing, of course.

Then a Delft blue ring tempted me. Across the Netherlands, we had seen Delft blue tiles, plates, vases, mugs, all large, breakable, and expensive. We had seen no rings.

I tried it on. It fit! The band was shiny silver. On its Delft inset a classic windmill towered over a tiny shed. A perfect memento!

The end of June was approaching. I had stayed below budget. "How many dollars?" I asked. With rolled r's and guttural vowels, the fifty-year-old shopkeeper replied, "Three dollars."

Only three dollars! I could afford it. It wouldn't break like larger tiles and didn't require suitcase space. I could wear it on my finger.

Would it keep its beauty? The Delft would not show wear. But what about the metal? Was it silver? I knew that some metals easily tarnish.

"What is it made of?" I asked, pointing to the band.

With a patronizing smile, the vendor said, "A metal." Why did she smile at me as at a child?

What metal? I wondered. I smiled my own patronizing smile. Her English vocabulary probably didn't include silver, nickel, or stainless steel.

I debated. I wavered. I took the plunge.

The next week, when the three of us flew back to La Guardia, we were proud we had not once gotten lost all month. En route to a night with my New York cousin, we took the wrong subway and ended up in Brooklyn instead of the Bronx. On the return subway, we laughed at the irony.

The silver coating of the ring band began to disappear in two weeks, leaving black marks on my finger each time I wore it.

Back in Iowa, when funds allowed, I turned in my film for developing: My camera had malfunctioned. Every photo was fuzzy, faded, and useless.

Joyce and John fell belatedly in love a few years later. They married.

During those same years Marlo and I met and married.

The ring's silver color has totally disappeared. But its brass tone is consistent, and leaves no finger marks.

When the Delft blue matches my clothing, I still wear the ring, and I remember my twenty-three-year-old self who bought it. Was she fearless? Naive? Perhaps both.

In the decades that followed, Marlo and I have made more trips. I have purchased souvenir rings that do not tarnish. But not one of them has a story that arouses more pleasure than this sole surviving memento from that fledgling adventure in 1971.

16 Guatemala Jewelry

"Look, Mabel, the hat pulls everything together and makes the costume," a customer says to his wife. I am volunteering at The Work of Our Hands, Pella's fair-trade store, during Pella's annual Tulip Time.

I take a deep breath and smile. "The hat is from the village of Volendam," I tell him. "It is the best-known of the different Netherlands hat styles."

I do NOT tell him how true his observation is. I have outgrown the rest of my Volendam costume by fifteen pounds. My long black skirt and matching shirt are twenty-first-century North American. My blue tulip earrings, made in Mexico, were purchased at this store yesterday. My scalloped turquoise necklace is from Guatemala.

Mabel admires the stuffed animals nearby. "Feel how soft they are!" I tell her. "It is like touching a cloud. I gave the llama to my granddaughter for Christmas, and it is now her favorite stuffed animal among many." Mabel picks up a unicorn, rubs its soft fur, and carries it with her as she does further shopping.

I wonder, *Is it really my granddaughter's favorite stuffed animal? I know she really loves sinking her fingers into its cloud of fur, but I don't truly know it is her favorite.* I could have just said, "And she loves it," which would have been more true. But the moment for truth has passed. I can't chase Mabel down and correct my statement.

I finger the tiny beads of my scalloped necklace and remember when the tourist role was mine in Guatemala and the merchants were street vendors, hawking their wares.

When the first jewelry vendor approached, I averted my eyes. She was undeterred. She pulled several samples from her bag and showed me.

"Only twenty dollar," she said.

I shook my head no.

"Fifteen dollar," she offered.

Again I shook my head. I already had a plethora of jewelry back home in Pella.

After I had declined her third offer, she walked away.

I second-guessed my decision. *Was I right to refuse her?* Our Guatemalan missionary friend had told us how people from surrounding villages made only a subsistence living selling jewelry to Guatemala City tourists. By comparison I was a wealthy North American. I could afford to buy her wares.

I was eating an ice cream bar from a food vendor when a second jewelry maker approached with intricate beadwork. She showed me a first, second, and third sample. The third caught my attention. It would match the turquoise earrings I had bought on a Navajo reservation in Arizona.

She read my body language and spread out the turquoise necklace on her hand.

"Twenty dollar," she said.

"Ten," I responded, to my husband's chagrin. He hated the bargaining. Knowing their poverty, he thought I should pay full price. I thought I should conform to the local bargaining culture and not appear to be a money-wasting rich foreigner.

"Fifteen," she said.

"Twelve," I countered. And she nodded.

"You buy another—just ten dollar," she offered.

I shook my head and paid her the twelve dollars. Guilt compelled only one purchase, not two.

She pocketed the money and went in search of a new tourist. The first vendor returned. Sad-eyed, she accused, "You buy from her but say no to me."

A long pause, filled only with my guilt and indecision, followed. She saw her opening. She pulled out a variety of colors and designs. One in black, gold, and brown was especially appealing.

"Only twenty dollar," she said. I bargained anemically and paid $15 for it. She rewarded me with a huge smile, although I thought her eyes remained a bit accusatory.

Back in Pella, I discovered the second necklace worked perfectly with a black turtleneck, and I wore it often. The turquoise necklace had languished in the jewelry box for five years—until this year's Tulip Time.

Six months ago, the images of the jewelry vendors still lurking in the back of my conscience, I began volunteering at Pella's fair-trade store as a long-distance vendor for artisans in the developing world. The work assuaged a little of my wealthy-tourist guilt.

Today, as Mabel and her husband leave the store, stuffed llama in hand, I wish there were an equally productive way to assuage my white-lie vendor guilt.

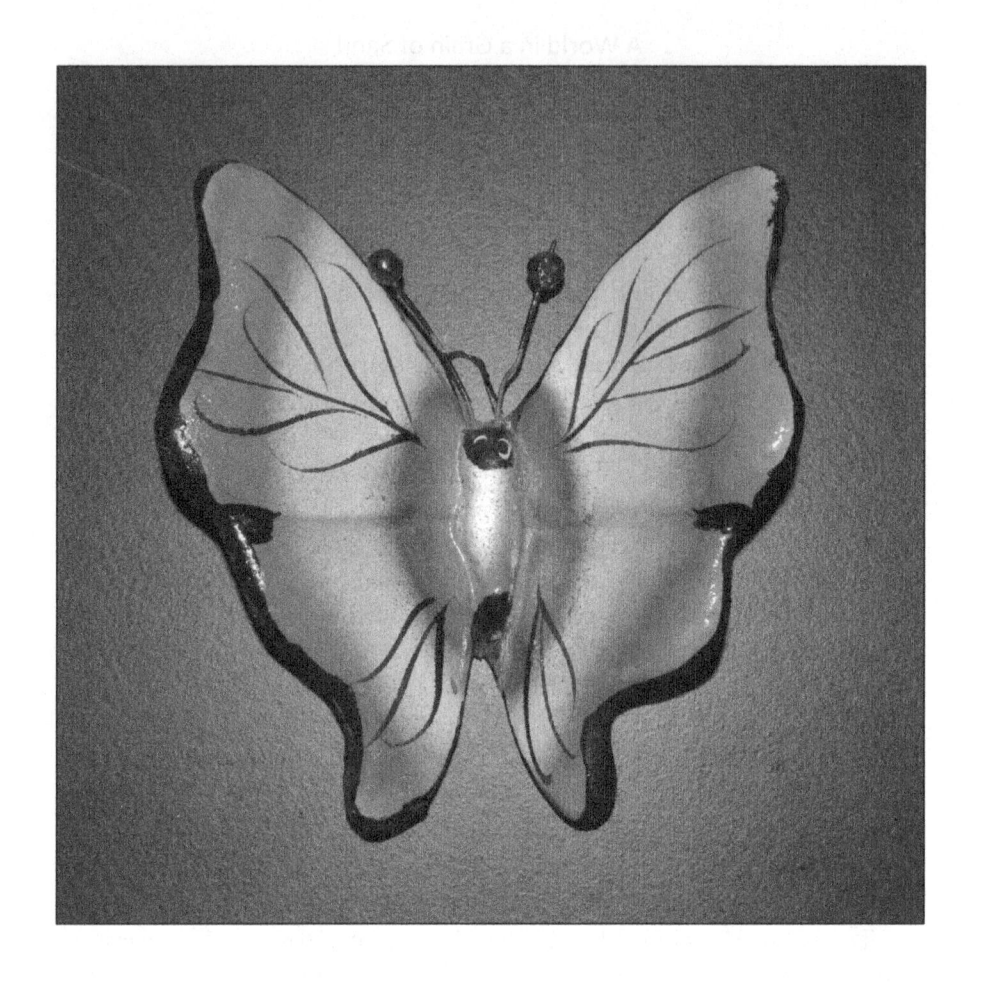

17 Mended Wings

On the dresser near my workstation rests a six-inch ceramic butterfly. It was handmade, wood-fired, and painted by an artisan in Nicaragua. Although I have met the creators of several of my Nicaraguan ceramics, I have not met the maker of my butterfly. It was a gift.

During my fourth trip to Nicaragua, Juan Granados approached me as I admired a similar ceramic butterfly perched atop a large, cement mushroom on the grounds of the Nehemiah Center in Managua, where I was part of a short-term mission team. Juan worked as the center's business manager.

"*Me gusta* (I like it)," I said in my rudimentary Spanish. "*De donde está* (Where is it from)?"

A World in a Grain of Sand

"*De Masaya Mercado* (from Masaya Market)," he responded. Later that day I learned the Masaya Market was an hour from the Nehemiah Center, too distant for a drive during our 10-day volunteer trip. I erased a butterfly souvenir from my mental wish list.

However, on the day of my departure, a smiling Juan presented me with a ceramic butterfly. He had made a trip to Masaya and purchased it for me.

I thanked him profusely. His thoughtfulness in making that trip to buy it touched my heart. Knowing his income as a native Nicaraguan was just a fraction of my husband's and mine, I treasured his generosity even more.

I carefully wrapped my gift in layers of capris and T-shirts and placed it at the center of my suitcase for the flight to Iowa.

Back home, I opened the suitcase on my bed and stripped the clothing from the butterfly, eager to find a place for it on my shelving. I groaned when I saw it. A wing had broken off, probably when one of those husky baggage handlers tossed it a couple of yards under the pressure to meet flight deadlines.

"Look!" I moaned to my husband, Marlo. "Juan's butterfly is broken. It's ruined!"

A mechanical engineer and a glue expert, Marlo tried to soothe me. "It's not totally ruined. I can glue the wing on. It will be almost as good as new."

He took the ceramic butterfly to his garage workshop and performed his magic with epoxy and clamps. After it dried overnight, he returned it to me, with its wing reattached. Although the crack in its wing showed, the butterfly remained beautiful.

I put it on the chest of drawers near my desk. I began to enjoy its mended beauty.

My first couple of trips to Nicaragua, I had gone as part of a short-term mission trip. Subsequently, Nehemiah Center Director Joel Huyser asked me to write a book about the center's work in Nicaragua, and I agreed. On subsequent mission trips to Nicaragua, I researched the country and the work of the Nehemiah Center. Nicaragua had poorly functioning political, economic, and police systems. Nicaraguan Christians at the Nehemiah Center knew their country was broken, but they believed they could work together to improve the lives of Nicaraguan people. So did the North Americans who worked alongside them. Living out their faith in their lives, they mended Nicaraguan society and culture, piece by piece.

My broken, mended, and still beautiful butterfly became for me a symbol of the work of the Nehemiah Center in a broken and beautiful country. I chose *On Mended Wings* for the book title. A photo of my broken and beautiful ceramic butterfly appeared on the book's front cover.

On Mended Wings was published in 2011. In the years since then, the ceramic butterfly remained on my office chest of drawers. And I have begun to see myself in it as well. I have gone through multiple breaks and mendings. I have been broken by my own wrongdoing and weakness as well as grief, illness, disappointment, and aging. I have been mended by forgiveness, surgeries, medications, therapy, accountability groups, devotional reading, prayer, and worship. Some of the glued places remain visible; others have disappeared.

Across the years, the breaks and mending happening in me have also occurred in others. As we broken-and-mending people work in our gardens, hospitals, schools, and governments, we mend our broken world as well.

When Juan gave me the ceramic butterfly on that day years ago, he had no clue what it would come to mean to me.

Neither did I.

Neither do any of us when we make gifts, mourn breaks, and follow inner promptings to mend God's broken and still beautiful world.

18 Left Behind

Within two minutes of entering the house for the first time, my husband Marlo stared at the gap between the kitchen cupboards and the ceiling, and exclaimed, "Carol, the pottery from our sun porch could go right there!"

We were looking for a home to which we could downsize.

The realtor smiled. He later told us that when clients begin picturing their possessions in a space, their interest level is very high.

He had reason to smile. Within two days we owned that home. And now a row of ceramic vases perches above the simple birch cabinetry. Each of the thirteen vases is different. Some feature flowers, butterflies, birds or turtles. Others have geometric shapes—angular lines or spiraling swirls. All were handmade by artisans in Nicaragua. And all are left behind.

Ten years ago, Marlo and I began making annual trips to Nicaragua with volunteer teams from our church. On one trip we visited San Juan de Oriente, a village of five thousand people—the vast majority of them potters.

We watched one of them throw pots in a one-room workshop attached to his cinder-block home with corrugated steel roofing. With bare feet, he powered his potter's wheel, shaping his wares with consummate skill. After the pots dried for several days, his family members primed and glazed the pieces. Using tools created from bicycle spokes and other bits of metal, they etched in lines and chipped away bits of clay to create relief designs. They then fired each item in a wood-fueled adobe oven in their backyard, starting at lower temperatures and eventually firing at an estimated 825 degrees for several hours. The next day, when the ceramic pieces had cooled, each was carefully removed and polished with a cloth.

Start to finish, the process required twenty-two days.

This process we witnessed was repeated in similar workshop-homes throughout the village. As we walked the village streets, stopping at shop after shop, Marlo and I were moved by the beauty of their products, by the glow of pride on their faces as they showed us their process—and by their hand-to-mouth daily subsistence.

We wanted to help. We thought, "We can surely find buyers who would appreciate the fine craftsmanship and beauty of the products of San Juan de Oriente!"

We made a series of purchases. In all, we enthusiastically purchased hundreds of attractive ceramics—vases, plates, luminaries, urns, and more.

Our plan: invite friends, acquaintances, and fellow church members to a preliminary sales event. Then subsequently sell ceramics from a craft tent at Pella's annual Tulip Time, which attracts a hundred fifty thousand tourists each May.

By the end of the first Tulip Time, we had sold twenty percent of our inventory.

Sales were sluggish at subsequent, smaller craft fairs, and at subsequent Tulip Times. Discouraged, we realized that our first-year sales had been primarily to friends and acquaintances—and they were definitely not an ongoing market.

We discounted the pieces significantly. Then we started giving them away as birthday and Christmas gifts.

In the end, we eked out a marginal profit. However, we earned far less than minimum wage. And we grew weary of slogging uphill for sales. We had less stamina than the Nicaraguan artisan families.

At the end of six years, we stopped selling and gifting altogether. What is left behind—pieces equally as beautiful as those we sold—provides beauty above our kitchen cabinets. When I eat a sandwich at the kitchen counter, I often survey the pottery. What comes to mind, however, is not the tough slogging toward marginal success.

Yes, these pieces have been left behind. But the vivid memories of slow sales have long faded.

What comes to mind instead is the glow in the wood-fired kiln. What stands in memory is the sparkle in the artisan's eyes and the lilt in his voice as he told us about digging the *barro* (clay). It is the shape that magically arose on the potter's wheel under his clay-stained fingers. It is the careful precision with which his daughter chipped out bits of pottery to create a relief design. It is his wife's pride as she showed us the shelves of drying shapes. It is the knowledge that each piece is the result of a twenty-two-day, hands-on labor of love.

Over the years, the pieces have morphed from leftovers to legacy. And I am grateful to the artisans of San Juan de Oriente for adding beauty to their world and mine.

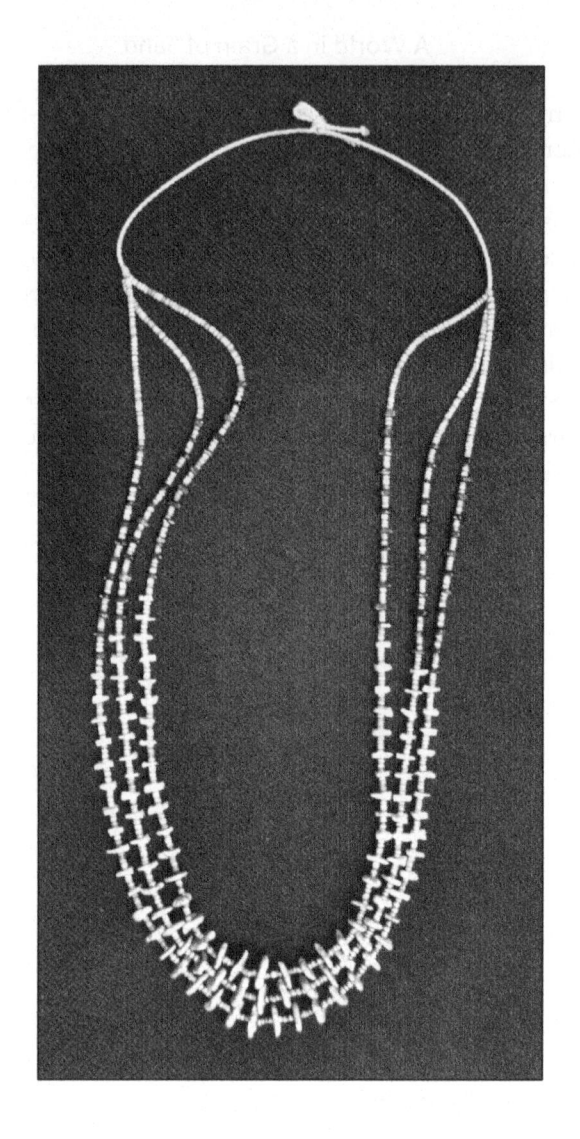

19 Valuable Turquoise

Today, I select my three-strand turquoise necklace from my jewelry table. The stones contrast nicely with my dark sweater.

Twenty years ago, two members of a Navajo church choir from Rehoboth, New Mexico, gave the necklace to me during their concert tour in the Midwest. Whenever I wear it, I think of them.

A World in a Grain of Sand

When my friend Rose, who grew up in Rehoboth, first saw it, she informed me it was valuable. I knew turquoise was important in Native American culture, but I didn't know my necklace had value.

Later, I wondered about my friend's assessment. I searched the internet for the value of genuine turquoise and saw necklace prices of hundreds of dollars. My necklace was beautiful, but I doubted it was genuine turquoise. The choir members we hosted were not wealthy women.

As I slip the necklace over my head, I remember transporting those women from our church to our home where we hosted them overnight. They stared through our van windows, saying in amazement, "How green. How green!"

I thought, but did not say, "Of course, it's green. It's June in Iowa." I found their fascination strange.

That winter I traveled to Phoenix. As we drove through the New Mexico desert, I stared through the minivan window at the mesas and sand, and I said to my husband, "How brown. How brown!" Now I understood our guests' fascination with Iowa grass.

As I check my appearance in the mirror, I remember the choir's arrival by tour bus. According to the itinerary they had sent, they would arrive at 6 p.m. By 5:45, our congregation had a hot dinner buffet ready. The hands on the fellowship hall clock ticked past 6:30, then past 7:00. We kept the food warmers burning. We received no phone calls. At 7:30 the choir cheerfully arrived. We awaited an explanation. We expected a profuse apology. They provided neither.

We were a little miffed—and confused. How could they be so-o-o late and act as if nothing unusual had happened?

The next week I told Rose the story. She nodded, smiled, and said she had experienced the same as a child. Navajo culture did not place the same value on punctuality.

"Why not?" I wondered.

I searched for it online.

I learned traditional Navajo culture views time as cyclical, not linear. Different from my culture, it doesn't obsess over progress or punctuality. Things will happen when they are meant to happen. Navajo culture places a greater value on relationships and on staying until the present moment is complete.

I grudgingly accepted this different-values reason for their lack of concern, but I saw my values as superior.

A World in a Grain of Sand

A year or two later, on a volunteer vision-and-learning trip, I was plunged into Nicaraguan living, where time values resemble those of that Navajo choir. When a worship service was scheduled to begin at 10 a.m., hardly anyone had entered the sanctuary by 10. Between 10:10 and 10:30, church members started to saunter in while a sprinkling of worshipers belted out praise songs. The new arrivals invested time greeting each other warmly before they walked to their seats.

Being late didn't matter. Worship would be done when it was meant to be done. Often it ran for two hours. I saw no one consult a watch, wondering about meeting their next deadline.

North American missionaries told me that when beginning business meetings, Nicaraguans paused to ask about the health of others' families. At noon, they lingered over communal lunches. In Nicaragua, North American businessmen said they never once heard the admonition, "Come on, hurry up! Time is money."

Nicaragua was my first experience immersed in a different culture, and I realized the assumptions I made about time were just that—assumptions. I stopped regarding my Western concept of time as superior. It was simply different.

That launched a new value for me: cross-cultural experiences. Via Zoom, I began helping a Cambodian learn the English he needed in order to work with international organizations in his country. I helped some Central American immigrants in Pella master English. And they helped me with my rudimentary Spanish.

Today, as I leave the house, I think of the presentation I will make to help raise funds for refugees soon to arrive in Pella from Guatemala. Their relocation to our town is sponsored and arranged by Pella Welcome Corps, an ecumenical group of Pella residents I joined six months ago.

Would I have joined those volunteers without the journey that began with these strands of turquoise and the learning that followed? Did that hosting and the gifting perhaps launch a personal journey?

I finger the turquoise strands against my sweater. They may not be expensive, but they have been valuable.

I remember the old hymn:
> "God moves in a mysterious way,
> His wonders to perform.
> He plants his footsteps in the sea
> And rides upon the storm."

Mysterious ways, indeed.

Section D:
Dramatic Moments, Personal and Historical

20 Dolphins of Hope

In my brass collection is just one piece I did not buy from my father: a pair of dolphins at play. I bought these dolphins on September 11, 2001, just after learning about the destruction at the World Trade Center's Twin Towers and the Pentagon.

    I heard the news accumulate in bits and pieces on the car radio as I drove home toward Pella from board meetings in northwest Iowa. A Boeing 767 had crashed into the North Tower. Seventeen minutes later the South Tower was hit by another plane. President Bush announced an

A World in a Grain of Sand

apparent terrorist attack. Then a plane crashed into the Pentagon. A fourth hijacked plane crashed into a field in Pennsylvania.

Alone on Interstate 80, I needed to hear a loved one's voice. I pulled off at the next exit and tried to call my husband. He didn't answer. I called my son Chad. In shocked tones we commiserated. We consoled each other and feared what lay ahead. Eventually we said goodbye, and I drove on.

At Des Moines, I needed a break from driving and stopped at a Disabled American Veterans' thrift store. Still numb with shock, I wandered the aisles seeing little, until the carefree beauty of pair of brass dolphins at play called out to me. Their bodies arched in a tandem jump, they appeared to be re-entering the water together after leaping above its surface. Their graceful curves matched, making space for each other as they dived.

In that moment, they became for me symbols of normalcy and beacons of hope. The Twin Towers were falling, but the dolphins continued to play. They were tarnished, but still filled with beauty and grace. I bought them, took them home, and immediately began to polish them. I stared at the TV and polished, stared and polished, as my cloth and hands grew black. The images of destruction, played over and over, burned into my brain. The towers collapsed, killing people inside, including firefighters and police. New York was engulfed in debris and smoke. When I finally turned off the television, the dolphins gleamed gold.

It's now more than two decades since 9/11, and those images still replay in my brain. So do the stories of heroism that sprouted like flower seeds in the days that followed.

When the first plane hit the North Tower, the PA system urged people in the South Tower to stay at their desks. Rick Rescorla, head of security for Morgan Stanley, took a megaphone and instructed them instead to evacuate via the stairwell. Walking down the steps with them, he calmed them singing songs on the megaphone. When 2,700 people had exited, he went back in to check if more people were stranded on the top floor. Then a plane hit the South Tower, and it collapsed on him and others still in the building. He died, but he had saved 2,700 lives.

After the plane struck the South Tower, people on the 78th floor thought they were trapped. Then out of the smoke and wreckage appeared Welles Crowther, who led them to the only functioning stairwell, then returned again and again to lead others to the escape route.

When the tower collapsed, he was heading up the stairway to rescue still more people.

Two flight attendants called officials during the hijacking of Flight 11, which later hit the North Tower. They calmly and professionally gave officials the hijackers' seat assignments and other details that allowed officials to trace the hijackings back to Osama bin Laden in the days that followed.

Heroes multiplied as story after story of bravery and self-sacrifice came to light.

In the early moments, the images of darkness ruled, but in the days that followed the stories of heroism, along with a pair of gleaming dolphins, became my rays of hope and light.

21 Lindbergh Bowl

A blown-glass bowl created by Pella artist Sheryl Ellinwood perches on the coffee table in my great room, between the leather couch and the fireplace. Its forest-green exterior contrasts with its mottled-reddish interior. In 2000, it was given to me by the play cast and crew after the final performance of *Wings: The Lindbergh Story*. I named it "Lindbergh Bowl."

Wings was the second play Mary Meuzelaar and I coauthored. Four years earlier, the idea for a Lindbergh play had been born as the two of us sat on the Pella Opera House stage after the closing night of our first play, *The Dominie's Wife*. "Let's write about the Lindberghs next," Mary suggested. "Their story has everything: drama, heroism, and a fairytale romance. It is the great American love story."

I nodded. *Their story also included tragedy,* I thought. An infant son, their firstborn, was kidnapped and died.

We did some preliminary research, and we were hooked. In 1928 Charles Lindbergh, a good-looking American pilot, made the first-ever solo flight across the Atlantic and instantly became a global hero. After that flight, he and Anne Morrow met, fell in love, and married after just four dates. Anne then accompanied Charles on flights around the globe, until she eventually stayed home to raise their five children.

When completed, *Wings* was staged at the Pella Opera House. Then Mary and I moved on to other performance projects, satisfied with a job well done. Maybe after a few years, we would re-stage it, we thought.

Then on August 3, 2001, news broke: Charles Lindbergh had fathered three children with a German mistress. In 1957, at age fifty-five, he met and began an affair with hatmaker Brigitte Hesshaimer. Over the next seventeen years he flew to visit her two or three times per year, under the pseudonym Careu Kent. His mistress's children eventually learned his true identity but promised their mother they would not reveal their father's identity while she lived. After she died in 2001, they were free to tell the world their father's name. DNA tests confirmed Lindbergh's paternity. By the time the news broke, Anne Lindbergh had died, apparently without knowledge of his affair.

The scandal grew.

Subsequent months revealed that Lindbergh had also fathered two children with the hatmaker's sister and two with his German secretary and translator. On his trips to Germany, he spent time with all of them. All three women knew about the others and apparently tolerated the situation.

Our play had missed the mark! Charles Lindbergh was a hero with clay feet.

I comforted myself that A. Scott Berg had not discovered these indiscretions either when he wrote a 688-page Pulitzer Prize-winning biography, *Lindbergh*. And Berg wrote with full access to the Lindbergh papers! Berg did note, though, that Lindbergh seemed driven by a compulsive need to travel in his last two decades.

Charles Lindbergh, the great American icon, proved to be a fragile idol. As I gradually learned this news about him, he toppled and shattered into a thousand shards. I felt numb, betrayed, and then crushed. So much for the great American love story.

I thought again of the play and of Berg's biography. Were both now fiction?

Not really. The heroism, the romance, and the tragedy were real. But I now knew, as radio commentator Paul Harvey so often said, the rest of the story.

Mary and I never re-staged our play. When I donated my play scripts to Pella Historical Society, I omitted *Wings*. The hole in the story was too huge. My conscience, and perhaps my pride, did not allow me to include it in my writing legacy. Lindbergh's transgressions, like his life, loomed large for me.

There were moments when I was almost disgusted enough to shatter my Lindbergh Bowl. But I didn't. It remained beautiful. It remained a reminder of the drama team that worked together on *Wings* and of my friendship with Sheryl Ellinwood.

As my disgust dwindled, I realized we never know the whole story for anyone, not even for those closest to us. We all have secrets we don't tell the world.

Maybe Lindbergh fell farther than most, though. Then again, maybe he didn't. Maybe he lies shattered because I imagined him so high.

My Lindbergh bowl remains intact. I study it again and think of Sheryl and of the team that staged *Wings*.

I think again of Lindbergh.

Forgiveness begins.

I decide to rename the bowl.

I rechristen it "Grace."

22 The Gift of Words

On the shelf above my desk sit two volumes of *The Compact Edition of the Oxford English Dictionary*. It is called compact, not because it has a reduced number of words, but because of its reduced print size. Four pages of the normal-size OED have been shrunk to fit on a single page of the compact version. The words are so tiny a high-end magnifying glass is required to read them.

I did not buy these volumes; they were a gift. In 2019, I was working on a young adult novel whose main character Laura, a gawky and bookish thirteen-year-old, had a love affair with words and their histories. She looked up each new one she met in the OED, which has extensive word histories in addition to definitions. I lamented my lack of easy access to the OED to my writing group. I was astonished when Lee Collins, an octogenarian member of the group, offered to give me hers. She no longer used it, and she was in the process of reducing her possessions. The volumes did require a magnifying glass, and I would have to buy one. Hers had long ago disappeared. Was I interested?

YES, I was interested. She gave me the volumes, and I bought a lighted magnifying glass. I began investigating the words that fascinated the character Laura, writing their definitions and histories in my notebook.

Shortly after Lee had given me the volumes, *The Professor and the Madman*, a movie about the creation of the OED, was released. Before you conclude the movie might be bookish and boring, let me explain.

It features two men who appreciate words and word histories: Editor James Murray and contributor Dr. William Minor. To gather quotations demonstrating the use of words, OED Editor James Murray seeks volunteers. He finds them. Many people who love words and their histories offer to research word origins, perusing countless books for a word's earliest use.

The most prolific of those volunteers is Dr. William Minor, who lists his address as Broadmoor Criminal Lunatic Asylum. Murray assumes Minor is a physician at the asylum. After accepting Minor's excellent work by mail for nineteen years, Murray is astonished to learn that Minor is not a staff member, but a patient. In one dramatic moment in the movie, convinced his penis is the cause of his madness and "impure thoughts," Minor cuts it off. While he recovers, his submission rate plummets.

For column readers who are word lovers, here is my summary of the more academic information from the book *The Professor and the Madman*, on which the movie is based. In 1879, when London's Philological Society launches the project, the estimated completion time is ten years. After five years, the word definitions have reached only to "ant." Timeline revision is necessary. The ten volumes are finally completed forty-nine years later in 1928, containing 414,000 words. In the decades that follow, editors make revisions and additions.

Now, in 2024, the OED is also available online for a $100-per-year subscription. Experts project that by June 2037, OED will have one million words.

When Lee gifted me with her compact OED volumes, I thanked her and wondered what I could give her in return. The answer came from Amazon. My purchase of the magnifying glass entitled me to a second one free. I inquired about Lee's interest, and she said yes, she could use a magnifying glass. Small print was becoming difficult for her to read. I gave the second magnifying glass to her.

My dream of writing a young adult novel died a slow death. After several attempts and failures, I concluded writing fiction was not my gift. I would stick to crafting words in nonfiction.

Without that novel to work on, I had less interest. I am less interested in word histories than my fictional character. My use of the OED has shrunk to rare occasions. It is much faster to look up fundamental meanings of intriguing words in the online Merriam-Webster dictionary. Perhaps the time will come when I can gift it to someone who loves the history of words more than I do. I think Lee would like that.

For now, the OED remains on a shelf above my desk. It regularly reminds me of Lee's generosity. It reminds me nonfiction is my gift, not novel writing. And it reminds me of the gift that words themselves provide as I write and as I read.

23 Flute Player's Song

The Flute Player* has graced our home since Marlo and I married in May 1975. It is one of the few wedding gifts to survive the five decades since our wedding, unique among the bath towels, utensils, and frying pans we received as gifts. A heavy, two-foot sculpture, it was a gift from my brother Don Addink and his wife, Mary.

They married just four years before Marlo and I did, and they were a supreme example of opposites who fell in love. Mary was easygoing; Don loved precision. As a child, he spread his oatmeal on a plate, painstakingly leveled the cereal, and covered it with butter and sugar. He then cut it all into a grid of one-inch squares and forked it into his mouth, one perfect square at a time, without spilling a drop of butter.

Don relished math; Mary tolerated it. Don was academically gifted and debated intellectual issues vehemently. Mary had emotional intelligence and treasured harmonious relationships. Don hid his feelings; Mary shared hers freely.

Both of them, though, relished a hearty laugh at a good joke or a prank.

As Don's siblings, we Addinks shared many of his traits, so Mary provided needed balance at family gatherings. During one heated clan debate a few years after she and Don married, she blurted out, "Why do the Addinks always need to be right?" and fled the room in tears.

We sat stunned. When she regained her composure and returned, we provided no answer for her question. Some of us had never even considered other choices or behaviors.

After Mary was widowed by Don's death in a July 2000 auto accident, she continued to maintain close ties with us as her in-laws. She came to our family reunions. Along with my siblings and me, she took a turn helping to care for our father during his final months with lung cancer.

Each March after 2000, my husband Marlo and I made a winter getaway trip from Iowa to Phoenix. Each year, we spent several days with Mary. She and I discovered over the years we enjoyed reading the same books. To our surprise, our political loyalties made the same dramatic shift. Mary continued to share her inner world. And I discovered I could safely share my heart with her as well. Those visits were good therapy for both of us.

Occasionally, Mary traveled to see Marlo and me in Iowa. On one visit, I pointed out the Flute Player near the fireplace. "I have enjoyed her greatly over the years," I said.

I explained I liked seeing her lithesome lines. Over the years, gazing at her had become a source of grace and peace for me.

Mary and I paused together a moment, taking in her beauty. Together we admired her elongated body, slender fingers, and relaxed lotus position. Eyes closed, motionless, she focused solely on her silent song.

Then Mary said. "I'm glad you told me you enjoy her. I had just been thinking. 'What a strange choice I made for a wedding gift!'"

In early March 2024, Marlo and I enjoyed our usual three-day Phoenix visit with Mary. Following that visit, Mary and I texted each other a few times about the details of our days.

Now, in early April, my cell phone rings. The display says I have a phone call from Mary's son Jason in Phoenix. "That's strange," I think. "Mary calls me, but not Jason."

As I say, "Hello," my stomach tightens, with good reason.

Jason tells me Mary has died in the night, with no advance warning. I go numb. I stutter. I tell him how sorry I am.

I offer to call my siblings. He accepts. He shares a few more details of her passing, and our conversation ends.

I make the needed calls, repeat Jason's story, and leave my office for the couch facing the fireplace and the Flute Player.

"Mary died . . . Mary died . . . Mary died."

The words are a dream-like refrain from outside of me, struggling in vain to penetrate my brain.

I stare woodenly at the Flute Player. Today she provides no silent song.

At seventy-six, I have walked grief's path before. I know I have a rock-strewn journey to stumble through before my heart can hear once more the Flute Player's music of peace and grace.

---

*In several online locations the sculpture is identified as *Flute Player*, even though the musician's instrument more closely resembles an alpine horn. I opted to call her "Flute Player" because, for me, that term has more elegance than "Horn Player." The Flute Player sculpture was created by Dutch American artist Theodore (Dick) de Groot (1920-2019). My version of her was molded in plaster by Leonardo Art Works, Inc., in 1961.

24 The Memorial Stone and the Cross

A memorial stone lies in our patio garden, in honor of a young man I never met.

And never will.

Matthew Jay Rolffs, twenty-six, died in the middle of the night on May 26, 2016, in the front yard of our previous home.

My husband and I woke on a Friday morning to find our front yard filled with officers. An accident had happened during the night, the sheriff told us. He asked if we had heard anything. We hadn't.

A gray Honda Accord had missed a curve and slid sideways into our birch tree. The birch, shorn of seven feet of bark on the impact side, still stood erect. The car had split in half, the two parts stopping fifteen feet apart from each other. Under a draped sheet, its driver lay at the edge of a roadside flowerbed.

For the next three hours I watched our front yard through the sun porch windows, transfixed. Officials blocked the road, took pictures, examined the car pieces, marked tire tracks, used survey tools, and took notes. A few of the driver's friends and family arrived and watched motionless from the road. A pastor joined them.

One by one they left: medical examiner, ambulance, family, sheriff, deputies, detective, tow truck, and at length, the two highway patrolmen with their survey tools and camera.

I opened my front door and tiptoed through the yard. A few tire tracks scarred it where the car had hurtled into our front yard and a few more where the tow truck had dragged it out.

A few sprays of orange paint marked crucial locations. The lawn looked far too normal for a site where in the night a gaping hole had been ripped in time and space.

My heart cried out for ritual. I ached for ceremony—something to mark a young man's unseen passing in the dark.

I walked to the backyard and tugged up the cross I had bought two years ago from a local artist, made from huge spikes of old railroad ties. A cross of giant nails, it had touched my heart. I moved the cross to the roadside garden and pushed it down into the orange paint that had marked the location of one end of the white sheet.

Over the weekend, I added a flag and an angel statue.

Then, I sprayed a wicker chair sky blue instead of the bright red I'd planned for it. I set the chair behind the cross and put a container of plants in it.

The crash had also scattered quarter-inch shards of broken glass from the car windows across our entire front yard. I vacuumed up the shards with our leaf blower as best I could and disposed of most of them. I kept a dozen or so larger pieces, not sure why.

Then, when a friend hosted an event for making memorial stepping stones, I embedded the shards in heart-shaped cement and placed the memorial stone among the other commemorative items. When I weeded the memorial area, I often paused and remembered Matthew's passing and the shock for me and those who knew and loved him.

When we downsized in 2020, I disposed of the blue wicker chair. Iowa weather had faded and broken it.

I moved the cross of railroad spikes and memorial stone with me. They sit in a small garden next to our backyard patio.

Now, as I sit on the backyard patio years later, the stepping stone and the cross continue to mark for me that shattering moment. They still speak.

The shattered glass says, "Life is fragile," and the enduring metal cross replies, "But eternity follows."

Section E:
In Memoriam

25 Remembering Joan

Peter Stuyvesant stands atop the dresser near my desk—not the man himself, of course, but a four-inch miniature of him. Its details reveal the seventeenth-century Dutch governor's large nose, bushy eyebrows, feathered hat, and wooden leg. Governor of New Netherland (later renamed New York when conquered by the English), Stuyvesant was strong-willed and autocratic. His character resembled that of Joan Liffring-Zug who gave the miniature to me in honor of my Dutch heritage, she said. She had received it as a gift from the Museum of the City of New York, and, I think, considered it kitsch.

I first crossed paths with Joan in the early 1980s while in search of a photograph. Visiting the Amana Heritage Museum, I had discovered the Iowa Amana colonies ran day care centers before the rest of the country. As a writer and a mother of toddlers, I wanted to investigate that topic. The museum director suggested I contact Joan, who managed the Amanas' photo archives.

I mailed Joan a letter of inquiry, introducing myself as an article writer in search of a photograph. A week later, I received her response. She didn't answer my question, but she inquired about my writing experience on Penfield Press letterhead.

"Look, Marlo!" I exclaimed. "She's a book publisher asking about my writing experiences. I think this might lead somewhere."

It did.

I became the writer-researcher for *Delightfully Dutch*, a book of Dutch-American historical information and recipes that joined the Penfield Press line of books about US subcultures. According to the publishing contract, I would receive a royalty for each book sold.

When, a few years into our relationship, Joan described me as "incredibly parochial," I stuffed a retort, nodded, and tried to change the subject.

A proactive business owner, Joan took charge of all Penfield books and also of each of our conversations.

Two more Dutch recipe books followed, these for a flat fee, not a royalty. Joan explained Penfield needed to streamline its bookkeeping. The second two books were simpler and easier, so I agreed to the revised arrangement.

I continued my subservient role.

Until I didn't.

When Penfield decided to switch *Delightfully Dutch* to a flat fee payment instead of a royalty, I raged, "Joan wants to increase profits for Penfield and reduce incomes for her writers."

I telephoned other Penfield writers, trying to rouse them to united action. I failed. In the end, I succumbed.

Joan and I rarely communicated thereafter. We went our separate ways.

I started my own business, The Write Place. We helped businesses and social services with news releases, newsletters, and internal communications.

Then we entered new territory. We helped writers self-publish books. Our writer list grew. Tracking their data became complicated. My understanding of Joan's decision to simplify Penfield Press's relationship to authors grew. Perhaps my response to her decision had been a bit parochial.

On October 16, 2023, I learned somewhere on Facebook Joan had died one year earlier in a nursing home at age ninety-three.

Today, six months later, I stop keystroking at my desk, glance at Peter Stuyvesant atop the chest of drawers, and Joan comes to mind.

I search online for her obituary. It describes her as "Iowa's premier photographer." She first worked as photographer and editor for the *Cedar Rapids Gazette*. As typical in the middle of the twentieth century, the paper released her when she became pregnant. At the end of that pregnancy she became known nationally when she photographed herself giving birth in 1951. She added to a successful career in photography in 1979 when she launched Penfield Press. Over the next forty years her company published forty books and distributed them worldwide.

In an article in the *Iowa City Press-Citizen*, her daughter-in-law Carol Roemig-Heusinkveld refers to her as a "powerhouse of a person." I nod.

Then I find unfamiliar facts: In the 1960s, she used her photos and writing to oppose racism. Her grandson Forrest says she "had a soft spot for those who were unfairly treated, particularly women, minorities, and various ethnic groups." Of course, she considered me parochial! In the 1980s I was minimally aware of racism. I didn't think it existed in Iowa.

Then Forrest goes on to talk about her "rough upbringing," in which she shifted from living with one set of relatives to another throughout her childhood. He says her childhood led to "feelings of loneliness, unworthiness, and a motivation to prove herself by living an extraordinary life."

I stop reading and take a deep breath. I work to make this fit my image of her: A powerhouse of a woman, yes. But childhood wounds? Who knew? Not I.

I never did write the article I intended about the Amanas' Kinderschule. Joan never provided me with the needed picture or information.

It no longer matters. I take Peter Stuyvesant from atop the chest of drawers, and remember two other gifts from Joan, worth more than a daycare photo: a foothold in book writing and a larger world.

If Joan were alive today, I fear she would still call me a parochial woman.

But I hope she would concede I am a recovering one.

26 The Eagle and the Clematis

On my kitchen counter sits a small figurine: a bald eagle in front of a US flag. It is one of four eagles that were on the corners of my father's coffin. As his children, we chose these because we knew he would have liked them.

Dad was a World War II veteran and proud of it. For the back of his gravestone, he chose the words "Torpedoman's Mate 3rd Class"; the dates of his military service, 1943-1946; and the name of his submarine, USS Carbonero. He rose proudly whenever Navy veterans were asked to stand as a band played the song of their branch of military service.

Dad was a man of strong—some would say rigid—opinions. When his sons came home from science class claiming the term "vacuum" was a misnomer for a space with lower air pressure, the dinner table debate on the topic grew fierce. He insisted with equal ferocity that people who were members of our denomination which supported Christian school systems should leave our church if they didn't enroll their children in Christian schools.

Later, when his adult sons became computer experts, visited on holidays, and talked computerese with each other for too long, he announced, "Stop. It's time to talk about something else."

At ninety, he still retold the story of his first rent-for-shares landlord who insisted on receiving half of the shelled corn that fell beside the farm's grain elevator. "No other landlord expected half of that! It was supposed to be the property of renters," he insisted, irritated again by the memory and retelling.

Dad played cards intensely, complaining so loudly about bad hands and poor strategic decisions that some fellow card players—and my mother—were convinced he was angry. My brothers often matched their tone to his. One Christmas gathering, the disputes got so loud Mother told the card players, "Stop playing NOW! If you don't, I am leaving this house."

She meant it.

The game ceased.

In my youth, I rubbed up against his hard, military edges. Sometimes I opposed his views and tried to prove I was right. Other times I zipped my lip.

"Ain't the college ever gonna do a comedy?" he asked me, after several years of seeing me perform in dark plays such as *All My Sons* and *Antigone*. I concluded he couldn't appreciate good drama. I saw his distaste for the series of tragic plays I performed in as proof of his lack of education. And I was embarrassed he used the word "ain't."

Then I entered adulthood.

On an extended-family ski outing, Dad and I—the weakest of the adult skiers—paired up for easier skiing. Together we rode the ski lifts on the gentler slopes. Once, a panorama of sunlit snow, tall evergreens, mountain cliffs, and blue skies opened before us. After a moment of awe, Dad pointed with his ski pole into the vast beyond and said almost reverently, "Look at that. It's the reason I ski."

In 1984, he stood with me beside the crib of my three-day-old son, who slept as we watched. Though rarely demonstrative, Dad put his arm around me. "I'm happy for you," he murmured as he hugged me. His tone and hug told me he, too, was remembering the son who had died inside me two years before.

As he aged, Dad became a flower gardener. He sometimes invited me outdoors to admire the flowers that surrounded my parents' retirement condo. He relished them and pointed out special features as he watered. He especially enjoyed his purple clematis. "Look how tall it is!" he said. "And look at those flowers!" Against his white trellises, they were a profusion of purple.

The spring after he died, I spaded out a chunk of his clematis. After a few years, it bloomed profusely against my white trellis.

When my husband and I later moved to a retirement duplex, I took both the clematis and the eagle with me. Both continue to spark memories of Dad. These days, both the eagle and the clematis bring me joy in remembering him, and the paradox within him.

The paradox within us all.

27 Sunday Purse

Talking on the phone on a Saturday evening, I needed to tell a church newcomer how to recognize me in the church foyer the next morning.

I paused. Tall? Gray hair? Glasses? None of those would work. There would be dozens of women fitting that description in the church foyer.

Then I knew. "I'll meet you at the door that opens to the parking lot. I'll be holding a black and silver drawstring purse."

The next morning, that caller beelined toward me. I was the only woman present with a purse matching my description.

My purse is at least fifty years old. It first belonged to my grandmother Marie Huisman Kiel, who died in 1984 at age ninety-one. She had long hair, which she always swept back, fastened with hairpins and a hairnet. Wearing a black, knee-length dress and carrying this crocheted purse, she attended two services each Sunday at Orange City's First Christian Reformed Church. She entered through the west door and sat in a middle bench.

Her purse was small, but it had just enough space for cash for the offering plate, a lace-edged handkerchief for possible sniffles, and some peppermints to help stay alert during the 30-60 minute sermon.

My best guess is one of her eleven children gave it to her. The crochet threads are much heavier than the ones she crocheted with. And I don't think she had access to purchasing the metal cones that cap the purse's drawstrings. However, she likely crocheted the lace edges on her white handkerchiefs herself.

During my childhood, she kept two jars of peppermints (one held pink, the other white) in her kitchen. Whenever we grandchildren arrived, she smiled, opened her cupboard, and offered us a choice of colors. I often hesitated. We called both peppermints, but the whites were strong mints and the pinks were mellower.

The purse I use on weekdays is five times the size of hers, which was inherited by my mother and then by me.

I fill my weekday purse with the multitude of paraphernalia I am convinced I need to leave home in the twenty-first century.

For Sunday worship, though, I prefer just essentials, and I use my grandmother's. I carry some sugar-free cough drops to stop my nodding off or to prevent a potential cough.

Instead of a handkerchief, I add a couple of tissues for my sniffles. Did I inherit my allergies from her? I don't know. I did inherit some of her lace-edged handkerchiefs. Decades ago, however, I hired a crafter to convert those dainty squares into Christmas tree decorations.

I don't need to carry money in my Sunday purse. My husband, Marlo, carries that in his billfold. But I do add something that would astound my grandmother: my cell phone.

She reached middle age before landlines linked the rural Midwest. Farmers shared the lines. Neighbors could eavesdrop on each other's conversations. A human operator linked the callers. Grandma recognized her calls by the number of long and short rings she heard. When long-distance calling became possible, it was expensive. She rarely used it.

I have not yet reached ninety-one, as she did. But Marlo and I now have our own grandchildren. Last week Marlo answered a cell phone call from Elise, our twelve-year-old granddaughter. She wanted to learn about his youth for a school essay. She asked him about his childhood memories: family, games, religious practices, and then his earliest memory.

He answered Elise at length. I even learned new details about the multi-building fire on his family farm when he was five.

Elise concluded by asking in what ways the world had changed during his lifetime. He instantly responded, "Oh, Elise, there are so many!"

After a pause in which he tried to choose one option and to avoid the choices that would make him sound like an old fogy, he said, "I guess I'll choose communication."

He explained the dramatic shift from letter-writing to fax, email, computers, and smartphones. He said that his talking to her in Michigan from a car in Arizona would have sounded like science fiction in his childhood.

Listening to his conversation, I insert my cell phone into my huge weekday purse, and wish my seventh-grade teacher had given me a writing assignment like Elise's. I want to know more about Grandma Kiel's early years and about the huge changes in her life and world.

I conducted no adolescent interview with her. I have no word records of her childhood memories, just my memories of her in later life.

Each Sunday morning, when I insert my cellphone into my grandmother's small purse, I call her to mind. I remember her gentle modesty, her quiet dignity, and her unswerving devotion to her family and her God. My memories may be small, but they contain a treasure.

28 Aunt Gert's Afghans

I have two afghans, both decades old. One is pristine, and the other is well-worn. Both were crocheted by my Aunt Gert De Groot.

The pristine cream-colored one is identical to those of my siblings and cousins. As I recall, over time Aunt Gert crocheted identical afghans for all twenty-five of us. When I was twenty-one or so, Aunt Gert bought about three thousand yards of yarn, crocheted for twenty to forty hours, and gave the result to me. Over the years, it has consistently been folded across the foot of a bed in my home, and it shows no wear.

A few years later, as a newlywed, I wanted an afghan to match my living room furniture. At my special request, Aunt Gert crocheted a maroon and blue one from yarn I bought for her. She must have told me how many skeins to buy because I surely wouldn't have known, and Google was still decades in the future. Marlo and I—and eventually our three sons—used it as a lap blanket in our living room over the decades. Its stitches are matted and worn. If Aunt Gert were still on earth, she surely would offer to make me a new one.

Born in 1911 in Sioux Center, Iowa, Gertrude Addink was the oldest sister of my father, Henry. Single until her 40s, she lived with my grandparents long after her six younger siblings had married and left the nest. She helped on the farm and took charge of cooking for the three of them. Then John De Groot, a neighborhood bachelor, courted her. Early in their marriage, the pair lived with Aunt Gert's parents. Then Grandpa and Grandma Addink retired to town, and the couple stayed on the farm. (When newly arrived in town, Grandma needed to relearn baking. I remember she served us a few scorched cakes while she remastered the skill.)

When both of my grandparents died, their will provided for an extra $2,000 gift for Aunt Gert. They said the gift expressed their gratitude for the years she assisted them on the farm, and they wanted her to be able to afford a house when she and John retired.

Aunt Gert rarely laughed or raised her voice. She was easygoing and rock-solid dependable. When my mother once told me she had difficulty making conversation with Aunt Gert, I was puzzled. I found her company pleasant and comfortable.

When I was seven, my mother went to the hospital to give birth to my sister Kathy, her sixth child. I spent a few days at Aunt Gert and Uncle John's home. I remember its worn linoleum, wooden table, and steep stairway to my upstairs bedroom. Although my aunt and uncle were just in their mid-forties, I saw them as ancient.

Like most of her sisters, Aunt Gert was heavyset. One morning, I went outdoors with her to get water from the outdoor well. As she raised and lowered the pump handle, I was riveted by the loose skin flopping beneath her upper arms. (Who am I kidding? I wasn't just riveted. I was horrified.)

Uncle John was thin and silent. But when he ate soup at lunch, his slurping reminded me of the water from their outdoor pump. Having been repeatedly scolded for even the gentlest slurping, I held high standards for adult manners. I glared at him, wide-eyed and judgmental. I didn't dare criticize his transgression aloud. I wondered how his wife could tolerate it.

Grandma Addink had tended the chickens until she moved to town. Now Aunt Gert was in charge of both the coops and the kitchen.

I liked to help Aunt Gert gather eggs from the chicken coop each day. It made me feel grown up. But I didn't like the smell of hen-house disinfectant or feces. I was astonished by poop on some of the eggs. I had only seen the gleaming white ones in grocery store cartons. The hens clucked and complained as Aunt Gert reached gently under each of them to gather eggs, but they didn't deter her.

When Uncle John died, Aunt Gert moved to town, paying for her modest home in part with the money from my grandparents' will. As she aged, walking grew difficult. Hobbling on arthritic knees, she grasped at kitchen counters and armchairs to ease her walking. I never heard her complain.

When I last visited her, she was in a wheelchair in Sioux Center's nursing home. She asked me to open the bottom drawer of her dresser and choose a few hand-crocheted potholders to take home with me.

I gladly obliged, and I used them until they were in tatters.

I have only a few similarities to my aunt. I now possess my own flopping upper arms. And Marlo and I have downsized from a house in the country to a duplex in town.

I am also different from her. But I am not yet heavyset.

I once tried to crochet a square potholder with YouTube instructions. It contorted into a triangle.

My aunt was more generous than I am. I fight an instinct to hoard.

I am no rock. I do not have her easygoing and dependable nature. I struggle to subdue inner lightning and thunder.

I covet a few more of my aunt's genes.

Although she left earth long ago, she's still teaching me.

29 Aunt Kathryn's Blanket

A piecework blanket, reclaimed from brown, green, and yellow wool coats, functions as my guest room bedspread. It is too small for that queen bed, but I refuse to part with it.

Kathryn (Kiel) Wassink, my mother's sister, sewed it decades ago. When she died in 1999, her children gave it to my mother, who passed it on to me. Aunt Kathryn was only a year older than my mother, and they both inherited their ski-slope noses from my Grandma Kiel.

Both Mother and Aunt Kathryn had sewing machines, and both women were frugal. Mother sewed patches on my brothers' jeans, and lengthened or shortened them as my brothers grew and eventually passed them on to the next-born. She repaired ripped seams in shirts and blouses. She let out hems on skirts. With seven children under age twelve and a Spartan budget, she didn't have time for other sewing.

Aunt Kathryn had just three children. I suspect she also patched and hemmed. But I know she made piecework blankets like the one I eventually inherited.

Each year, Mother planted a single row of zinnias in her vegetable garden. Acquaintances have told me of growing up with a similar single row of zinnias. I think Mother saw the row as a gardening obligation that made her garden acceptable. She did not voice pleasure in it.

A World in a Grain of Sand

I don't remember a single zinnia entering my childhood home. Each stood guard from the front row of our garden for the entire season until it mildewed and froze, and my father finally hacked it down with the rows of frozen bush beans and cucumber vines.

Aunt Kathryn's garden abounded in flowers. My memory is emblazoned with a vivid video of her. Under a bright sun, she wears a wide-brimmed hat and gardening gloves, wields a clipper, and walks with peace and pleasure amid a late-August profusion. She gathers buds and blooms for indoor vases. In the fall she will dry some species for longer-lasting arrangements.

The Wassink home was spacious with an entire room dedicated to Aunt Kathryn's sewing and flower arranging. In childhood I concluded the Wassinks were wealthy. Our sewing machine was crammed into the corner of the living room. My siblings and I jammed together in scarce bedrooms. I never considered that their house size was the result of Uncle Arend's occupation as a house builder.

Mother laughed easily but was also quick to shout or cry. Apparently, she also had been a volatile child. At six, I asked her about the vivid four-inch scar on her forearm. The first time I asked, she said, "I burned it on an iron."

A few years later, she confessed the truth. "It is forever a reminder of the terrible child I was. I was angry with Kathryn. I chased her through the living room and crashed my arm through the glass pane of our French doors."

Mother raised us to fear what neighbors thought of us. Her externalized standard asked, "What will people think?" That question often lit the path for our family choices. Aunt Kathryn, however, exuded self-respect and quiet dignity.

The whole Wassink family was less volatile, competitive, and verbal than mine. In early adolescence, I once traveled in the back seat of the Wassink car to a shared two-family vacation in Minnesota. Without competition, I filled the airtime with stories and jokes. The Wassinks listened, nodded, and laughed. It was glorious!

When we arrived at the rustic cabins on the shores of Dead Lake, our two families explored our separate cabins, unpacked, and rejoined late afternoon. Aunt Kathryn and Mother chatted as they prepared an evening meal for twelve.

"Is your cabin OK?" asked Mother.

Aunt Kathryn hesitated, then said, "It's fine . . . But the bedroom for Arend and me has bunk beds."

A World in a Grain of Sand

She wrinkled her nose.

"Really!" Mother exclaimed. Then she offered, "Hank and I can switch bedrooms with you halfway through the week."

I knew just enough to realize their conversation had a subtext. They expected sex! I held my breath.

"No, it will be fine," Aunt Kathryn insisted.

Was she sure?

Yes, she was sure.

They stopped talking. I resumed breathing. Then I realized that in the night this week my aunt was going to climb out of her single bunk, snuggle with my uncle in his, and—

I wrinkled my nose.

My aunt hadn't used the word, but she had dared to talk to my mother about sex—a taboo subject in our home. When I had once used the word "sexy," Mother declared, "I don't want to hear you use that word again—ever."

When Marlo and I married in 1975, Aunt Kathryn created artificial flower arrangements in the *klompen (*wooden shoes) I had purchased and painted for our reception tables. For decades, I displayed a pair of the arrangements in my home. I donated them to a thrift store during our 2020 downsizing.

But I kept Aunt Kathryn's blanket.

Over the years, she filled the same wife and mother roles as my mother and other women of their generation. I never heard my aunt or mother utter a single feminist sentence.

But within the ancient structure, Aunt Kathryn found dignity, identity, and creativity. I realize that over the years, I have moved toward those same values within a more feminist frame.

I see her again, bending and clipping blooms, making time for the flowers that filled her with pleasure. I remember her dedicated room providing space for the crafts she valued.

And I am grateful.

30 Stillbirth Weaving

An embroidery hoop frames a circular weaving on a wall near my desk. I named it "Stillbirth Weaving." I created it thirty-nine years after my son Craig was stillborn.

In 2021, I was one of the speakers at "Beauty from Ashes," a retreat for parents who had recently experienced the stillbirth or death of an infant. Retreat organizers asked me to speak because they wanted attendees to hear from someone looking back on the experience after decades had passed, to recall not only the pain but also the healing associated with the passage of time.

Just before my presentation, Angie Van Roekel from Garden Chapel Funeral Home led the grieving parents in making a circular weaving in memory of their deceased baby. Decades after Craig's stillbirth, I was no longer grieving. I participated in the exercise to show solidarity with the young parents who were aching with grief.

I chose yarn colors to match those in the blanket of the bed in my office that doubles as a guest bedroom. Then I wove them in a circle, beginning with the dark brown and transitioning to lighter and lighter colors until I ended with a fringed, creamy yellow. I didn't think I would want to hang it, though. After all, thirty-nine years had passed.

Soon it was my turn to present. I told those grieving parents about Craig's growing quiet that last week of my pregnancy, about the undetectable heartbeat, the ultrasound, the news of his death in my womb, and his subsequent birth in a delivery room that was deathly still. We heard no baby's first wail.

In the weeks that followed, my overriding question was "Why?" Sometimes the cry was accompanied by guilt. I thought maybe I had not been a good enough mother. Sometimes it was accompanied by self-pity or jealousy. I asked repeatedly, "Why me?" Other women I knew were giving birth to living babies. Sometimes I asked the question out of anger. One afternoon I drove to the cemetery. I sat in my car with the windows closed, and shrieked, "Why?" It was a primal scream from the core of my being.

In my grief, I read my way through the book of Psalms, and there I met my own laments. Seventy percent of the 150 Psalms contain lamenting in which the writers cry out to God in pain. I made those Psalms my prayers.

Amid all my "why" questions, I read this sentence by Harry Emerson Fosdick, "Persons can put off making up their minds, but they cannot put off making up their lives."

That sentence became a crucial touchstone for me. I had two other sons to care for. Life around me was not going to stand still until I had received an answer to my question. As I walked through the darkness, putting one foot ahead of the other, there were pinpoints of light from the counsel of other women, who said through tears, "I lost a baby, too."

A cousin told me, "It does get easier, but you never forget."

Over time my "Why me?" question shifted toward "Why not me?" When I entered the world of grief, my eyes were opened to the pain of those who surrounded me. Everyone at some point experiences pain and loss. I began to shift toward gratitude for God's good gifts—my sons, husband, family and friends, sunrises, sunsets, a morning cup of coffee . . . They were all gifts. I did not create or earn a single one.

As I shared my story at that 2021 retreat, the pain in the room was palpable. The parents' attention was laser focused. I felt like a pinpoint of light amid great pain. It was the first time I had publicly told that story, and I told it as a tale of memory, not one of current pain.

Arriving home, I was ready to put the weaving in the closet, but decided to try it next to my desk instead. After all, it matched the blanket on the bed. And I liked how it had turned out, with its image of the growing light from its center to its circumference.

It is still there. Whenever my gaze rests on it, the only word to describe its effect on me is "comforting."

My cousin was right. It does get easier with time, but you never forget.

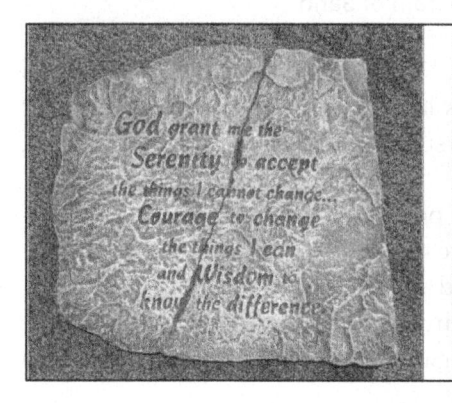

31 Serenity Prayer

I don't remember the first time I heard or read the Serenity Prayer, but I do remember it struck me as both beautiful and wise. I didn't memorize its words, but I identified with its contents.

Then my husband Marlo and I were slammed by our son Matt's telling us he was an alcoholic.

The Serenity Prayer embedded itself in my core as I recited it weekly at Al-Anon meetings with other relatives of alcoholics:

> God, grant me the serenity to accept the things I cannot change,
> courage to change the things I can,
> and the wisdom to know the difference.

Weekly for several years, I heard fellow Al-Anon members describe through tears the stories of their inability to change their addicted loved ones and their journeys toward acceptance. I cried too as I told stories of Matt's driving while drunk, his failed attempts at sobriety on his own, and his relapses after release from treatment programs.

I also found truth in an anonymous revision of that prayer:

> God, grant me the serenity to accept the people I cannot change,
> courage to change the one I can,
> and the wisdom to know that it's me.

Perhaps the anonymous author of that revision intended it as wit, but for me it became sanity-saving truth. My behavior was the only behavior

I could change, not Matt's. Not ever since his birth. But especially not after he became addicted to alcohol.

I also learned a broader lesson. Blurred boundaries damaged my other relationships as well. I saw my ache to control those I loved. I prayed the Serenity Prayer for those relationships as well.

Al-Anon stories, along with treatment center training and my therapist, told me often I could not rescue him. Intermittently and with great pain, I learned the wisdom to tell the difference between the things I could change and the things I could not. Although we made mistakes, Marlo and I found the courage to set our personal boundaries. We set our standard for life in our home: sobriety. To live with us, Matt needed to abide by the house standard. Eventually, he failed to meet that standard. He moved out.

A year or so later came a shattering phone call from a Des Moines coroner. Just two hours earlier, on July 16, 2017, 4:15 p.m., Matthew Van Klompenburg, age thirty-three, had died while sitting on his front steps. A next-door neighbor saw him slump over and attempted CPR without success.

A subsequent dose of naloxone by police also failed to revive Matt. Unknown to us, Matt's addiction had recently expanded to drugs. Cause of death: a combination of heroin, prescription drugs, and alcohol.

We went numb, then wept. We buried him and wept some more. I prayed the Serenity Prayer. Over. And over.

One group of friends gave Marlo and me a memorial garden stone with the words of that prayer. We placed it in our flowerbeds. Did those friends know its significance in Alcoholics Anonymous and Al-Anon meetings? During the early days of loss, it was too painful to ask. And then I decided the moment to ask had passed. I have never inquired. I do not know.

I do know the memorial stone comforted me often as I gardened. It reminded me friends grieved with us. It reminded me of the hard truths I had learned in Al-Anon and therapy, truths I still needed to relearn from time to time.

Somewhere in that blur of early grief, I bought another Serenity Prayer memento. I no longer remember where. I only remember I stumbled upon it used, either online or at a thrift store. It had already comforted some anonymous owner.

When new, it had been made from an upcycled book. This new-to-me memento with the Serenity Prayer could comfort me indoors, in addition to the reminder in my gardens.

Years passed. The garden stone cracked in two. Over the blur of years, neither Marlo nor I remember which of us stepped on it and broke it. I took a picture of the broken stone, and we parted with it. It had done its work. It was no longer an essential part of our comfort.

The memorial book, however, still sits in my office as a reminder of the son I loved, still love, and still grieve from time to time. I will never forget him.

The words on the memorial book remind me of the need for boundaries with my loved ones still on earth. I hope I never forget that either.

Section F: Epiphany Moments

32 Butterfly Visit

Two metal-and-glass butterflies brighten our bathroom. Both of them were gifts, one for Mother's Day and the other for my birthday.

In our previous home, with its extensive gardens, they hung outdoors, the larger one on a white latticework under the deck and the smaller one on a tree in the entry garden. They came indoors in winter for protection from ice and snow. One is made from molded metal sheets painted red, gold, and blue. The other is shaped from copper wire with molded plastic and marbles in shades of green.

In our home, additional butterflies are scattered throughout other rooms as well.

Why butterflies? It is not just because they are beautiful, although they are. My love of butterflies harks back to the day of a visitation by a monarch.

Sitting on my front yard patio decades ago, I tried to focus on the day's lectionary readings. The pages of my zippered Bible lay blurred and bright on the mosaic table. I squinted to block the midmorning rays.

Grasshoppers leapt from the azaleas. Crickets chirped. Under the August sun, moisture beaded up on the wrinkles in my arms. I sighed and gazed wearily at the sagging barn across the road. A monarch flitted from a milkweed pod, then hovered near me.

It had been a dry month in my gardens and in my heart. Times of meditation or prayer were followed by empty longing. As the monarch hovered, my longing rose. I sat immobile, willing her toward me, in silence begging her to land her curved triangles of orange framed in black on my freckled hands, my blue veins large under translucent skin.

As if in prayer, she flitted, teased, and then I held my breath as she landed on my wrist. She opened her wings, a black lace fringe at the rear of each. She folded them and showed me their lighter underside. Unfurling her black thread tongue into a wet wrinkle in my wrist, she sipped daintily. She hovered and settled down for a second sip, her wings translucent in the morning light.

My skin tingled under her feet and tongue. In June, her coiled tongue had been the chewing mouth of a caterpillar. In September, she would have laid her eggs and died. But today, wings opening and closing in the morning sun, she sipped a third time from the rivulet in my wrist and then flitted into the blue beyond.

Some say that the flutter of a butterfly's wings can, in time, trigger clouds or sunshine a continent away. I don't know about weather changes in the other hemisphere. I do know that when a monarch landed on me, drank deeply, and then lifted her stained-glass wings, my heart soared with her.

That memory keeps me adding butterflies to my home. Butterflies have become sacred symbols, reminders of the morning a monarch visited, sent by the King.

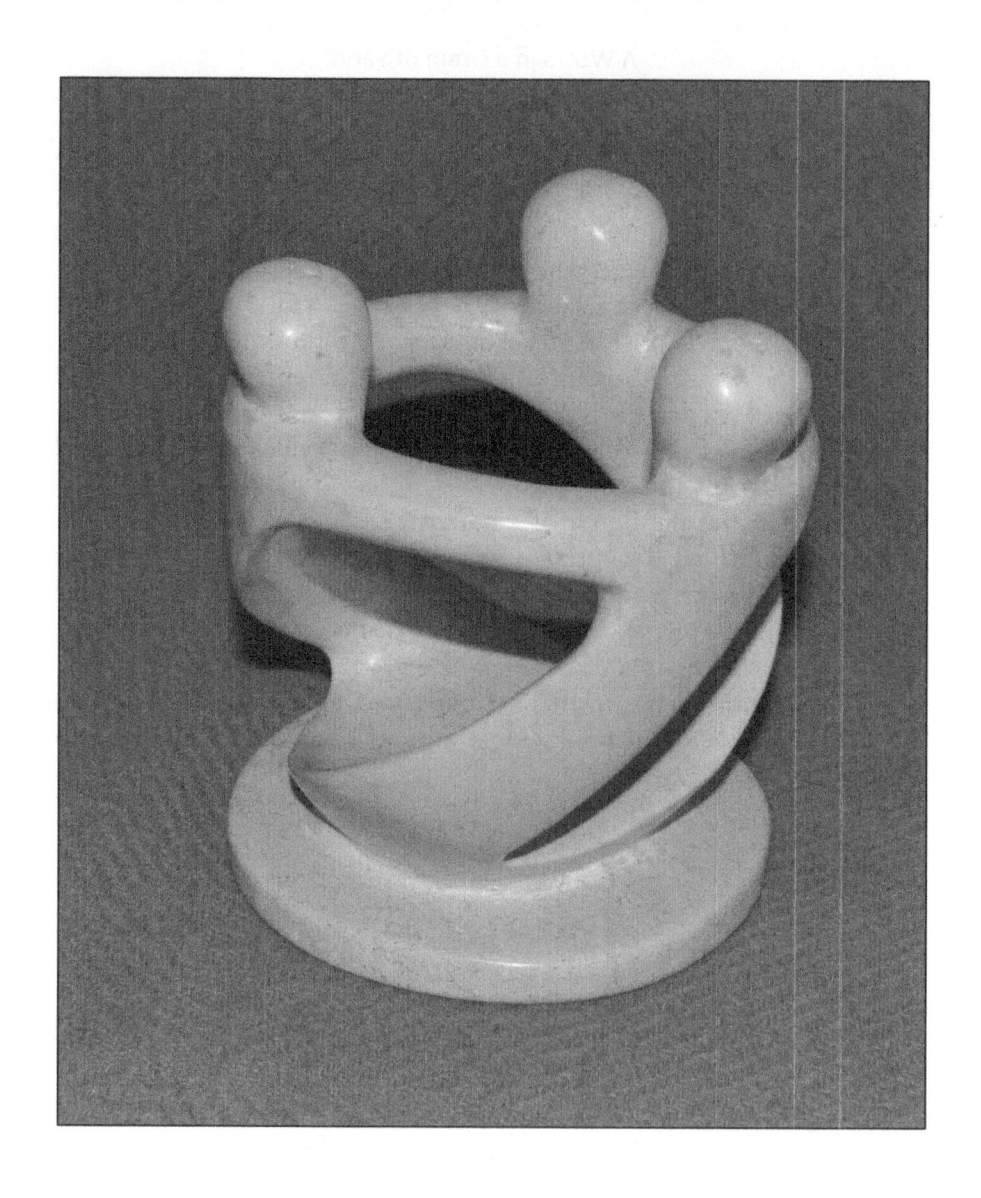

33 Friendship Carving

I don't remember how we got the soapstone carving with three intertwined figures whirling atop a single base. I think a sister-in-law who saw the three figures as a symbol of our friendship gave it to us.

Eventually, after several locations, it found a home on the shelf above my desk. Sometimes I enjoyed picking it up, feeling its weight and running my fingers over its smooth surfaces. I liked its minimalist simplicity and its reminder of friendships.

It was handmade under fair-trade conditions in the hills of southwestern Kenya. The fair-trade website tells me the workshop overlooks beautiful green hills. Artisans made the carving in stages. First they cut a large chunk and hauled it from a soapstone mine. They sawed the chunk into smaller pieces, then hacked it into a rough shape with machetes. They gave it more definition with chisels and other simple hand tools.

Then the sanders went to work, wet-sanding until it was perfectly smooth to the touch. Finally, the wet carving dried in the sun.

It sat on my shelf for years, always a symbol of friendship.

Then I was assigned a children's message for Sunday morning worship. My assigned topic: the Trinity. "That's a hard concept even for adults," I thought. "How on earth do I speak with preschoolers about it?" I sent the topic to my subconscious self for several days to see what ideas would rise. None did. I googled the Trinity and found complex theological treatises. Nothing useful there. I sat at my desk in despair, eyes wandering over the shelf, when my eyes stopped at the stone carving. It had three intertwined figures. I couldn't tell where the arms of one ended and the arms of the other began. And at the base, their bodies became just one.

I was tickled by the serendipity. I had my children's message.

On Sunday morning, I said to the children, "I have something to show you today," and I showed them the sculpture.

I showed them the base, and I asked them, "Is this one?"

I showed them the three figures at the top and asked, "Or is it three?"

They were perplexed. "If you look at the bottom, it is one," I said. "And if you look at the top it is three. But even on the top you cannot tell where one person begins and the other ends. The same is true of God. God is Father, Son, and Holy Spirit. Three in one. A mystery like this carving..."

As I exited the service, carving in hand, our pastor looked at it and said, "That is known as the Dance of the Trinity."

I looked at him in surprise. I had thought I owned a friendship carving.

Back home I googled "Dance of the Trinity" and found a Greek Dance of the Trinity tradition called *perichoresis*. At Greek weddings three dancers go in circles, faster and faster, until they become a blur. There individual identities become part of the larger dance. The website told me the early church fathers and mothers looked at the dance (*perichoresis*) and said, "That's what the Trinity is like."

I had not invented my explanation after all. I only discovered what was already there.

I think again of those Kenyan carvers. Did they know about the Dance of the Trinity as they sawed and sanded?

I like to think they did.

34 The Last Supper

A copy of Leonardo da Vinci's *The Last Supper* is one of three paint-by-number oil paintings I created in my childhood. It is part of a collection of pictures on our garage wall that are not attractive enough to display in our home, but are too precious to discard.

To paint the copy, I carefully matched numbered containers of oil paint to numbered spaces. I opened a tiny container and stirred it to mix in all the oil that had separated from the pigment. I then painted each shape with its number, let it dry overnight, and then selected a different color. It was a painstaking process for a ten-year-old. My parents had bought me the *Last Supper* project after I had completed two smaller paintings, portraits of a German shepherd and a cocker spaniel.

Like Leonardo, I did not work continuously on the painting, but I did complete it in one year. Leonardo worked on his far more detailed original from 1495 to 1498. My copy is just eighteen by thirty-six inches. His mural measures fifteen by twenty-eight feet.

Leonardo's mural has covered a wall in the dining hall of a monastery for centuries. My copy hung in my parents' dining room for just a few decades. Ownership reverted to me when my mother downsized to an assisted-living apartment.

Leonardo's arrangement of the disciples has taught me about taking artistic liberties. Jesus and his disciples are all on one side of the table. They are either standing or seated. Historically, they were probably reclining on both sides of the table. But, even at ten, I could see it made a more effective painting to have all thirteen people on one side of the table, mostly standing.

As I worked, I began to make connections with the picture. The faces in my copy were too rudimentary to speak to me. But I was touched by the disciple groupings and their body language. Some of the disciples were facing Jesus, simply staring at him. Others were conversing and gesturing in small groups. In the hand of one was a small bag. I concluded this was Judas with a money bag. In many disciples, there was a sense of tension and surprise. I decided this was the moment Jesus had just announced that one of these twelve would betray him. Later research confirmed my conclusion.

As an adult, I learned Leonardo identified each disciple in his preliminary drawings for the painting, and many of them have features that symbolically identify them. Peter has a knife: he would later cut off a soldier's ear. Thomas's finger is upraised: he would later use it to feel the nail holes in Jesus's hands. Judas's head is symbolically at the lowest level of all the disciples.

I remember in particular one moment of my painting process. I was recovering from a cold and home from church alone on a Sunday morning. Sitting at the dining room table, I opened a paint container, releasing the oily smell that had become familiar. I stirred it and carefully painted in some shapes. I was focused, lost in the moment, at peace. Later, in therapy, I would learn about the value of being fully present, and this was one of my earliest experiences of a moment of total peace.

Even now, stepping out of the car into the garage and pausing a moment to look at the painting can quiet me.

I no longer paint by number, but I do assemble jigsaw puzzles, and they have some of the same power to draw me into the moment. I focus on shape and color and piece size as a picture gradually emerges. When I walk away from a puzzle, I am more aware of the shapes and color variations in the world around me.

When I sit outdoors at a Pella city band concert, I feel the same slowing and the same sense of presence and focus as I do when looking at *The Last Supper*.

Slowing and being present are, I think, effects of art whatever form it takes. And it is the memory of that impact that keeps *The Last Supper* on my garage wall instead of in the trash.

35 Be Still and Know

"Be still and know that I am God" is stenciled on a framed board that I can see on the wall if I look up from my desk. It is one of just two items of decor in my office/guest bedroom that I made with my own hands.

I stenciled those words from Psalm 46:10 under professional guidance at a craft outing with friends and relatives a few years ago.

The word "still" is peaceful blue, "know" is green for growth, and "God" is gold because he is my king. The other words are a simple gray.

I no longer remember where I first read the suggestion of coming to inner stillness by repeating these eight words.

Although I don't remember where this phrase for meditation came from, I do remember the first time I met the concept of meditation-to-arrive-at-stillness. Decades ago, I read *The Relaxation Response* by physician Herbert Benson. I have read variations of his suggestions for meditation in many books since then, but his was the first, and it was a revelation.

Benson found four common components in the Eastern and Western practices that led to a relaxation response:

1. A quiet environment, which makes it easier to eliminate distracting thoughts.

2. A mental device, a repeated sound, a word or phrase, or a fixed gaze on an object. Attention to normal breathing is also helpful.

3. A passive attitude, which is perhaps the most important element in eliciting the relaxation response. Distracting thoughts will occur. Do not worry about them. When these thoughts do occur and you become aware of them, calmly return to the repetition of the mental device.

4. A comfortable position. This may be sitting in a chair, kneeling, or sitting on the floor in the lotus position. Lying down is not recommended because it raises your risk of falling asleep.

In the decades that followed reading Benson's book, I found multiple variations of meditation which elicited the relaxation response. I learned that this response reduced the fight-or-flight adrenaline rush and also lowered blood pressure.

One of those variations is Centering Prayer, as described by Fr. Thomas Keating. It is a prayer as a form of meditation, selecting sacred words or phrases that are repeated while slowly breathing in and out. (To see video instructions, search online for "Fr. Thomas Keating Centering Prayer Video.")

About the same time that I began practicing Centering Prayer, I read about using Psalm 46:10 as a quieting process. The instructions said to close my eyes and slowly repeat the words "Be still and know that I am God." I was then to repeat the phrase, omitting the last word "God." Then I was to repeat it omitting the second to the last word "am." I was to repeat this process, leaving out a final word each time, until all that was left was the first word, "be."

I repeated the phrase as a form of Centering Prayer. As I inhaled slowly, I mentally repeated the first four words of my sacred phrase. As I exhaled, I repeated the second four words. On each successive breath I left off the last word, until I simply said, "Be."

A World in a Grain of Sand

When I stenciled the words onto the framed board, I had been practicing Centering Prayer daily for several months, and it had quieted me. I have since moved on to other forms of prayer, but I continue to use Centering Prayer with that phrase when I am sleepless in the middle of the night. It stills my troubled thoughts and prepares me to return to sleep.

These days, whenever I gaze at those stenciled words from my office workstation and read the words slowly just once, I become still. I know He is God. And I am not.

36 Guardian Angel

During my childhood, a guardian angel picture on our living room wall brought me comfort as she guided a girl in a red dress across a deep ravine. The girl walks a narrow bridge, a log really, with a broken rail. She carries a bouquet and blue pitcher, apparently unaware of the angel alongside, arm extended, ready to catch her. The child's face is impassive, neither afraid nor confident.

The picture had been a wedding gift to my parents. They never parted with it. After they died, I chose the faded painting as a keepsake and hung it with other memorabilia on our white garage wall.

I used the picture in 2019 for a Sunday morning children's message during worship. It held the kids' attention well.

Today as I enter my driveway, NPR airs a story about a girl in Gaza, dehydrated and starving. I shudder. As I exit my car, I pass the guardian angel. "Where is the angel for that girl in Gaza?" I ask God. "Where is she for any Gaza residents?"

My questions continue. "And where was she that snowy day when that toddler just a block from here sledded downhill into the path of an oncoming pickup truck?"

My mind flits back to a recurring question: "Where was God the day my son died from a drug overdose?"

I stride into my office, plop myself at my computer, and decide to confront those questions. I promise myself honesty.

No words come.

I wonder what I told those children in my 2019 message. I click open the electronic file. I find a series of four versions of the picture that I created in Photoshop, each revealing successively more of the scene.

Suddenly, I am back five years in the middle of that message projecting images onto the church screen. I show the face of the girl in the red dress. "I'm going to tell a story," I tell the gathered children.

The next image reveals her dress, the flowers, and the pitcher. I ask what story it is telling. The children decide she is carrying flowers to her grandmother.

"Is it a happy story or a scary story?" I ask.

"A happy story," they say.

"It seems that way," I answer. Then I add the broken bridge and deep ravine. In Photoshop I have removed the angel.

They change their minds. "Oh! It's a scary story," they say. I agree.

I show them the entire image. I ask what is new. They tell me, "The angel!"

"Does that make the story less scary?" I ask.

Each of them nods yes.

What shows up next in my notes shocks me back to 2024 and my current darkness. According to my notes, I pulled out the actual framed picture and told the children this was a picture from my childhood. "The deep and dark ravine scared me," I said. "Looking at it and the broken railing, I was terrified. Looking at the angel, I felt safer. She reminded me that God loved me and took care of me."

I reassured them, "Even in the scary times, God loves you and cares for you."

Then I gave each of them a three-by-five photograph of the picture.

I am relieved I didn't promise them perfection or safety from all evil. We live in a broken world.

Nevertheless, this morning I have many questions and no easy answers. I know from long experience I will not find easy answers. I also know that hope will eventually return.

I think of another children's story, *The Lion, the Witch, and the Wardrobe* by C. S. Lewis. Lucy and her siblings enter the magical land of Narnia, where animals can talk. Lucy asks a beaver if the lion Aslan (a Narnian Christ figure) is a safe lion.

The beaver replies, "Who said anything about safe? 'Course he isn't safe. But he's good. He's the King, I tell you." The beaver doesn't explain or prove his statement.

Neither can I.

Some days I make it safely to the other side of the ravine. Today I have plunged into an abyss. I don't have satisfactory answers for my questions or an easy escape from the darkness.

But I can inch along in today's dark ravine, trusting that God is King, that God weeps with me, and that God is love.

37 Scarlet Ribbon

The past five years, two red ribbons have served as my Bible bookmarks for a weekly Lectio Divina (Divine Reading) meeting of six women. At 6:45 a.m. each Tuesday morning, we gather to hear two sections of Scripture, one from the Old Testament and one from the New Testament.

In the hour-long meetings, we pray for listening hearts, and then take turns reading aloud. We hear each of these readings four times. After the second, third, and fourth readings, we respond one person at a time to a question about the two passages:
1. What word or phrase shimmers for you in each passage?
2. Why do those words capture your attention, or how do they make you feel?
3. What do you feel nudged toward in response to this passage, or what do you want to ask of God?

If time allows, occasionally we read the passages a fifth time. We close by praying around the circle in response.

Established by St. Benedict in the sixth century, Lectio Divina was practiced in early monastic communities as a daily encounter with

Scripture. Its purpose was to lead readers into loving communication with God.

I first met Lectio Divina two decades ago at Emmaus House, a Catholic retreat house in nearby Des Moines. Reading Scripture this way at Emmaus House did lead me into that loving communication with God. I suggested beginning weekly Lectio meetings to my Pella friends. We have been meeting ever since.

And the scarlet ribbons?

I made one for each member the week after we read Joshua 2, in which Jericho resident Rahab helps Israelite spies escape death. They instruct her to drape a scarlet rope from her window and down the city wall beneath her home when the whole nation of Israel arrives. The Israelites march around the city seven times, the huge walls collapse, and the Israelites kill Jericho's residents.

The wall beneath Rahab remains standing. This gentile prostitute is saved because she has draped the scarlet rope down the city's protective wall.

As we read together, I was astounded to learn from a footnote that early Christians regarded that scarlet rope as an Old Testament symbol of the coming Christ.

The following morning, to remind myself of that symbolism, I bought two yards of red ribbon and cut it into bookmarks for each of us. I had enough ribbon for a second bookmark for myself.

Since then, when I have opened my Bible to our Lectio readings for the day, the bookmarks have continued to affect me in a way hard to find words for. The ribbons remind me of both Rahab and Christ. The scarlet cord saved her as Christ saves me.

My ribbons are not sacraments like Eucharist and Baptism, but they do have ritual value. They appear each time I open my Bible. They move with me through the pages from week to week.

The first few years of Lectio, I doubted the process I had launched. My Christian tradition places high value on an intellectual approach to the Bible and a correct theological interpretation of it. Sometimes in Lectio meetings we apologized for the message we heard in God's Word that day. We said, "This probably is not correct theologically, but today I hear..."

Nevertheless, over the decades of practicing Lectio, God communicated his love to us. When we responded to God, rote prayer formulas faded, replaced by a new authenticity. We also bonded with each other.

I don't have a sophisticated theology for what happened. But I felt the presence of God during those weekly meetings.

During those same decades, my enchantment with theology diminished. More recently that enchantment nosedived as I listened to theologians debate at length the Greek meanings of a single word. Their argument disillusioned me.

A few weeks ago, I bought a new Bible and a cover for it. I wanted a Bible with more room to write in the margins, and my current cover was tattered.

I considered options and chose a different translation from my current NIV Bible, the version most of the group members used. The variety would enrich our reading. I also searched until I found a wide-margin Bible that had extensive footnotes as featured in my old one.

Although the scarlet ribbons were also frayed, I kept them. However, the Bible and the cover both were shorter than my old ones. When I zipped the cover, the red bookmarks consistently jammed in its zipper.

Was it time for new bookmarks? The new cover provided attached black ones. I couldn't decide.

At the next meeting, as Ruth moved her ribbon from one page to the next, she smiled and said, "I remember when you gave these to us, Carol. It has been a long time..."

I did remember. I decided to keep the ribbons. Returning home, I trimmed their frayed edges and then shortened them a bit more. They no longer jammed the cover's zipper.

I am still searching for a new relationship to theology. I hate to hear holy words used as bludgeons. Perhaps, as Lectio continues, the Holy Spirit will nudge me forward in my relationship to theology as well.

Section G:
On the Lighter Side

38 My Father's Brass

My home is a brass menagerie. Rabbits, cats, and squirrels perch on the bedroom dresser. A buffalo, a crane, a camel, and a deer march in a row below the fireplace. Seventeen owls peer from the shelving in the great room. Flanking the entry are some larger pieces, just below the vaulted ceiling. A bull, lion, roadrunner, and pair of dolphins stand guard on one side. An assortment of vases adorns the other. Each of these items, sparkling throughout my home like glitter, is brass. Nearly all of them were purchased from my late father—after considerable friendly haggling about an appropriate price.

During Dad's first decade or so of retirement from selling Snap-On Tools, he crisscrossed the country as a short-haul trucker and as a Red Cross volunteer. Somewhere around age seventy-five, he switched gears and began rescuing brass—both in his hometown of Orange City and wherever he traveled to see one of his adult children, scattered across the country in five different states. He scrounged through garage sales, browsed Goodwill stores, and bid at auctions. No piece was too far gone for rescue, if the price was right.

He loved the hunt—and the thrill of bargaining for a rock-bottom price. "It keeps him young," my sister-in-law once said. I nodded. Indeed, it did.

Dad repaired and polished each brass purchase till it gleamed like gold. Brass is, after all, known as a poor person's gold. After a few enthusiastic months, however, Dad's basement workshop began overflowing with his rescues. He found an outlet: his three daughters. On our trips to Orange City, a few minutes after arrival, he issued the invitation, "Come down and see the brass!" That, too, was in a voice that brooked no argument.

In the basement, retired salesman that he was, he extolled the virtues of his favorite pieces. If my eye lingered on a piece, he immediately placed it in my hands.

Some pieces had stories.

The bull, for example, came from a Texas Red Cross trip. He had admired it on a client's mantel after he helped repair her flooded home. "You like it?" she asked. "It's yours. It's my thank-you for all you've done."

His price for me? $15 seemed reasonable to him.

"That's highway robbery considering you got it free!" I said. "I'm thinking more in the $5 range."

"But look at the quality!" he insisted. "It is one of the best pieces in this entire room—a bargain at $15."

He was right. It was the most carefully crafted piece in the room. But, of course I couldn't admit that.

He sensed my wavering and leapt in with more justification. "I have lots of labor invested in it. And think of the mileage transporting it back from Texas!"

"It's been a tough month," I said. "Could I pay in installments?"

"Sure, but I would have to charge interest," he retorted. "I think about $5 interest per month."

I pretended shock. "Isn't that illegal?"

"A man has to eat . . . and there is no state law about interest rates."

"But isn't there a Bible verse about the evils of extortion and usury?"

And so it went for each and every purchase, until we eventually reached a meeting of the minds on pricing.

Eventually, I specialized in brass owls. If Dad spotted an owl, he snapped it up. He knew he had a sure sale. My sister Kathy collected swans and tiny farm animals. Jan especially liked apples and bells.

The collection of brass, gleaming gold throughout my home, is a memorial. However, the owls remind me not of loss but of gift—the gift of my father's life—brimming with zest and energy, with laughter and love.

39 Mouse Phobia

Nine months of the year, a six-inch mouse sculpture sits on its haunches in my patio garden. Its tail spirals up around a rain gauge my husband and I check and empty after storms and showers.

My sister Jan gave it to me; she has an eye for attractive garden art.

I often smile when I spot it from my patio chair. I am surprised I enjoy it, considering my fear-filled encounters with rodents across the years.

The earliest rodent encounter I remember was my mother's, not mine. Our family of nine had moved into an old rental house on the edge of Orange City, Iowa. Cracks marred its foundation. Mice invaded often, and my father emptied traps weekly.

One morning I heard Mother scream when a mouse jumped at her face from our family's oven. She had leaned down and opened the door before igniting its gas-powered flames. Dad added a trap behind the stove.

Ever after, when Mother opened the oven door, she stood upright and at a distance.

One rainy fall day, ready to leave for school, I opened my boot and, just before inserting my foot, spotted six hairless, pink mouse babies squirming in the boot heel. I dropped both boot and contents. I ran for Dad. He emptied them into our trash heap. Did he also kill them? I never asked.

That Christmas season, I jolted awake to the crackling of a cellophane bag. On the chair next to my bed, a mouse nibbled a caramel in my bag of Christmas candy, just twelve inches from my nose. I leaped from the bed and ran downstairs. Dad added upstairs traps.

As a junior at Dordt College, I lived in a campus mobile home just across from an Iowa cornfield. Metal skirting with mouse-sized gaps surrounded its exterior, and a square hole surrounded round pipe in the floor beneath the kitchen cupboards.

When the weather cooled in fall, a mouse per day entered the kitchen via the square hole. With no resident father available, we coeds coped. I could set and bait traps with peanut butter; my roommate Joyce could not. But I lacked her stomach for releasing the squashed mice into our outdoor garbage cans, so she obliged.

My mouse revulsion increased when a summer college job included breathing nauseating rodent odors while deep-cleaning kitchen cupboards in which mice had feasted, multiplied, and defecated for months.

A few years later, I read about a man who became deathly ill with hantavirus after extensive contact with rodent droppings.

My niece Sabrina is a child with zero fear of rodents. She owns pet rats, each of them named. Dashie, a white rat with black spots and a gigantic tail, is her favorite. She often removes him from his cage and lets him sit on her shoulder. Not only that, she cuddles him and (ugh) kisses him.

When she offers to let me hold him, I cower across the room from her. I shudder, squeak "no thanks," and scurry from the room.

I am not alone in my mouse phobia. Google tells me nine percent of people are very afraid of mice, and another seventeen percent are a little afraid. Further internet research tells me the fear of mice is thousands of years old and is one of the most common specific phobias.

The fear of mice is partly a socially induced, conditioned response. In other words, my mother was afraid of mice, and I was exposed to that fear frequently. So I became afraid of mice. If exposure is repeated, as mine certainly was, that fear is reinforced.

In addition, fear of mice can originate in a startle response, a reaction to an unexpected stimulus. Spying a speedy mouse in my house is certainly unexpected and startling. I startle, and fear follows.

As I research rodent fear, I ponder. How can I enjoy my mouse garden art when my fear of mice is so ingrained and powerful?

I study my sister's gift again.

It is genuinely cute. Its face is round and friendly. It has no beady black eyes. No sharp front teeth are visible.

But its appearance is not what seals the deal for me. As I study it further, its tail and nose do not twitch. It does not bare its teeth. It cannot chew or poop.

Its most endearing quality of all: it is frozen in stone. It can never run toward me or attack me. I am safe from it forever and ever.

40 Bargain Clock

A battery-powered clock stands on the shelf above my desk. My father, Henry Addink, purchased seven similar clocks decades ago. As far as I know, he gave one to each of his children.

"Can you use a clock?" he asked me when I visited for the weekend. He showed me a choice of three styles. "I figured you kids can always use a clock. It has an alarm, too."

He grinned and added, "They were only two bucks at the K Products store."

K Products was a promotional merchandising manufacturer in Orange City, where my parents lived. The company sold overstocks through their outlet store at absurdly low prices. Bargain hunter that he was, Dad made regular trips to the store to search for new bargains—T-shirts, sweatshirts, pens, rain gauges, water bottles, key chains, thumb drives, rulers, calculators, and more.

"Are you giving them away or selling them?" I asked with a smile. When he had brass from a garage sale, it was for sale—not a gift.

"These I'm giving away," he said.

"Sure!" I said. If cheap was good, free was even better. I was, after all, my father's daughter.

Often, when I visited, Dad asked, "Want to go to the K Products store?"

"Sure!" I said. As soon as I walked through the entry door, I felt bargain fever. Our family had weathered years of poverty in which even bargain prices were out of reach. Dad and I thrilled as we touched trinkets we could buy at absurdly low prices. We could probably use this, and that, and that, and . . . We didn't need a guaranteed use. If it had potential use at some point in the mythical future, it went into the shopping cart.

Sometimes we made good decisions. The ink flowed from a bargain pen so smoothly, it became a favorite. But at another time, a keychain languished in a drawer until cleaning day when it went in a box for the local thrift store, Bibles for Missions, to be sold for an even lower price.

K Products was not the only place we hunted bargains. Dad frequented Goodwill stores across the country. I often stopped in at Bibles for Missions.

Approaching retirement, I considered volunteering to help sort merchandise in the Bibles for Missions donation room. Then sanity returned. I would come home laden with bargains every day I volunteered. I pictured myself on one of those hoarding shows, needing to clear a place on the table to set food, walking from room to room through narrow aisles bordered with towers of clutter. I volunteered instead as receptionist at a social service agency.

When my husband and I downsized to a duplex, we purged a third of our possessions. I kicked my garage sale habit. I no longer browse the garage sale ads in the local shopper. However, I still feel the tug when I see a handmade garage sale sign and a driveway full of potential bargains.

I must admit I did recently succumb and came home with a new-to-me purse. It cost only a dollar!

My father's gift became my alarm clock until the smartphone alarm era, when it moved above my desk. Now I rarely consult it, since I wear a wristwatch every day all day. It is 9:30 in the morning as I write this. I look up at the clock and see that it says 3:00. The battery has gone dead.

But I am not ready to part with it. When I look at it, I see my father grinning and saying, "It was only two bucks!"

41 Wren House

    Hanging near our house in the backyard is a fused-glass birdhouse. Like my other fused-glass items, it is the work of glass artist Sheryl Ellinwood. In 2020, after we moved into this duplex in Pella, I set the birdhouse on the ground next to the five-foot peace pole and a ceramic cactus. The neon blue and orange colors of all three blended perfectly. "I can't imagine a bird living in a house this beautiful," I thought.

In 2021, I hung it from one arm of our four-arm bird feeder. To my amazement, a pair of wrens made it their home. The male transported the twigs and straw for the nest structure. The female followed by creating a soft lining and sitting on the nest to warm the eggs. After the eggs hatched, both parents fed their babies. Between feedings, they sat on the arms of the feeder and sang their rapid, high-pitched, and amazingly strong rat-a-tat-tat melody.

However, the melodic warble became a fierce warning whenever other birds, most of them larger than the wrens, alighted near the feeders. The wrens successfully warded off many would-be diners, and we saw far fewer birds at the feeder that summer than we had the previous year. That dearth of birds persisted throughout the winter, long after the wrens had migrated.

In 2022 we were wiser. We hung the birdhouse on the opposite side of the patio from the feeders, at about the same height as the previous year. We prepared to enjoy the wren songs and nest-making again—along with a larger collection of birds at the now-distant feeder.

One week that summer, I saw a small brown bird perched on the peak of the birdhouse, and then another flew into the hole. I smiled with delight, then frowned. Those weren't wrens; they were sparrows. Grrr. Lowly sparrows. Sparrows who chirp instead of sing. Sparrows known for their messy habits and their overabundance.

Sparrows! Why did the sparrows find it before the wrens? Is there any way to get rid of them? Can I empty the nest and re-hang it? They will, I suspect, simply rebuild. I guess I will just have to grin and bear it. Sparrows. Sparrows!

To make things worse, five sparrows discovered the feeders. Five sparrows and not a single other bird. Five sparrows. That sounds familiar. I remember Luke 12:6: "Are not five sparrows sold for two pennies?" Given the plethora of sparrows in Iowa, I couldn't get even one penny for the five of them.

Then, unbidden, I remember the words that follow, *"Yet not one of them is forgotten by God."*

My birder friend Charlie has told me she enjoys sparrows. "Their chirping sounds so cheerful."

I listen. It does sound cheerful.

Today, in the absence of wrens, sparrows will just have to do.

Then, on the lawn, I spot a flash of blue and orange. Pecking seeds between the blades of grass, there sits a bluebird.

42 Puzzling Tale

During the COVID quarantine in 2020, my husband Marlo and I became jigsaw puzzlers. We ordered one from *Our Iowa* magazine, which Marlo reads cover to cover each month. The puzzle's picture: five spaniels in five beige crocks on a leafy field bordered by evergreen shrubs. It arrived in a cardboard canister and had 1000 pieces with the most irregular puzzle shapes we had ever seen: some abstracts, some animals, some large, and some tiny.

For past puzzles, we had hunted for rectangles with consistent protrusions and indentations. That process was impossible for these puppies and crocks. The project lasted days. We first joined edge pieces, then sorted the rest by color on a dozen homemade cardboard trays. Sometimes a tray tipped and spilled a few pieces. Sometimes an errant sleeve brushed a piece or two from the table edge. Whatever the cause, we instantly retrieved each of them.

Quick retrieval was essential: Marlo is a fastidious puzzler. As a teenager he once completed a puzzle and discovered a final piece missing. He snail-mailed the company. He wrote its staff he was certain he hadn't lost it, described the missing piece's precise location, and asked for a replacement piece. Instead, they sent him a new puzzle.

As we worked, the puppies and crocks took shape first, then the grass and autumn leaves surrounding them. Eventually only the black-green evergreens remained. As we placed the last pieces, we were dismayed. The puzzle lacked a final piece.

We looked around our chairs. We got on our knees and searched again, looking under chairs and table. We checked the entire carpet and examined the nearby shelving. We brushed through the folds of our clothing and then the clothing we had worn in the past week.

We puzzled over the missing piece. We could think of no other place it might be hiding. A mystery confronted us.

We waited a week or two, hoping the lost piece would miraculously appear, and finally gave up. We decided to glue the puzzle to poster board and frame it anyway, just as we had done with several recent puzzles that had no gaping holes. We had hung them on a finished wall of our garage. Visitors passing through the garage often paused to admire them.

We recreated the missing piece. The pieces surrounding the hole were almost pure black. I found black construction paper, traced the missing shape, and cut it out. Marlo glued it in place, along with the rest of the puzzle.

Above the dryer was an inconspicuous space, out of sight from visitors. We hung the puzzle there.

Months passed.

One morning, in a burst of cleaning enthusiasm, I removed my cell phone from the fanny pack I often wear at home to keep my phone near me. Then I emptied the fanny pack of accumulated tissues. Among the tissues appeared the missing puzzle piece.

Mystery solved! My sleeve had secretly brushed it there during puzzle solving. After cutting away the construction paper with a utility knife, we put the final piece in its proper place.

Now, we sometimes take guests to the laundry room to view the puzzle, complete with puppies, crocks, grass, and evergreens.

Of course, we not only show them the puzzle, we tell them our lost-and-found story, pointing to the wayward piece.

As they examine that piece, Marlo and I look at each other and rejoice again that the mystery is solved and the lost has been found.

43 Three Scenes with a Mobile

High above our entry door is an arched window. During sunny days, six strands of a fused-glass mobile glow from that window, casting colored shapes—crescents, circles, ovals, and diamonds—on the adjacent wall.

During our 2020 downsizing move, we removed it from the trapezoid window in the sunporch of our too-large home. I had little hope of finding a new location for the mobile. We would now have no sunporch or trapezoid window.

After we settled in, however, we considered that arched window. Marlo did the math and concluded we could hang the strands there, in a different order, and they would display well.

He sketched a plan, then put some screw-in hooks and a pencil into his pocket. Carrying an electric drill, he cautiously stepped from the top of our ten-foot stepladder and onto the narrow ledge below the window.

Age 73, he reached up and stood on tiptoe. He could just reach the window's arch, nineteen feet above the entry floor. In that position, he marked locations, drilled holes, and turned in screws. After climbing down the ladder for a break, he re-climbed it and placed the mobile strands one by one on the ledge. He stepped onto it again.

Six times he reached down, picked up a strand and strained upward to hang it, careful not to step backward and plummet to the tile below.

Safely back on the entry floor, he sighed and said, "I don't think I will be going up there again. I am getting too old for this."

. . .

While I was brushing my teeth one morning, Marlo called from the kitchen table, "Carol, come here. We have a bird in the house!"

When Marlo had opened the back door to greet the morning, a sparrow flitted in.

Together we shooed the sparrow toward the open door. Instead, it scurried further in and then took flight. As it searched for open sky in the kitchen, the great room, and under the vaulted ceiling, I watched for falling poop.

The bird spied the arched window, beelined toward it, and perched on its sill. It pressed against the pane behind a red piece of fused glass.

We yelled, we waved our arms, and we whistled. It continued to hug the glass. Then it walked along the sill, looking longingly at the trees and grass.

We looked at the floor-to-ceiling distance. I thought about the ladder. Nope. We couldn't even catch it at floor level. It would be suicidal for a seventy-four-year-old to ascend to the heights, shout, and wave his arms to scare a bird out of that window from atop that narrow ledge.

"I'm calling pest control," I said in my no-nonsense voice, marching toward my office and the phone book.

Marlo stayed put. Trusting Marlo wouldn't fetch the ladder in my absence, I closed the door to prevent a sparrow invasion. I dialed

A World in a Grain of Sand

Menninga Pest Control, reached voicemail, and left a breathless message about the bird: I needed pest control STAT.

I stayed put and distracted myself with email sorting because I did not want to witness any havoc that creature might be wreaking in my house.

Ten minutes later Marlo called, "Carol, come here! I got it!" While I had distracted myself and waited for a return call, Marlo had plotted. He had fetched our shop vacuum with a v-e-r-y l-o-n-g hose and covered the end of that hose with bird netting. He then duct-taped the hose to the telescoping pole we normally used to change ceiling bulbs. Turning on the vacuum power, he used the pole to lift the hose toward the cowering sparrow. He poked the hose between the mobile strands, trying to pin the sparrow to the netting with suction.

I scurried to the entry to discover the bird imprisoned against the netting with Marlo slowly lowering the hose toward the floor. I opened the entry door and inch-by-inch Marlo extended the hose through it. He closed the door against the hose and turned off the vacuum.

Released from the netting, the bird sat on the sidewalk, dazed. After a few trembling wing flaps, it flew to a nearby elm.

Marlo grinned and said, "Guess you need to cancel that phone call."

. . .

Despite Marlo's poking and prodding, the glass mobile had remained intact. Behind it, though, our house sparrow had released some ugly streaks of frustration.

Eventually the bird-in-the-house trauma faded, and I began to want that window cleaned.

I called a professional window cleaner.

Marlo, now seventy-five, didn't even consider standing on that high ledge to scrub bird dung from the window. And, after careful thought, he had failed to invent a way to wash it using a shop vacuum and a telescoping light bulb changer.

That technique was for the birds.

44 Chili Contest

I am terrified of church suppers.

No, that's wrong.

I am terrified of making food for church suppers. My mother was, too.

I am a plain-Jane cook, a food minimalist. I treasure ease, speed, and efficiency. I buy precut salads, microwave frozen vegetables, and warm up store-made mashed potatoes.

I keep these habits hidden. I hate exposing myself publicly as a below-average cook.

You see, since kindergarten I have been competitive. I hate being below-average at anything: being chosen for a recess sports team, Iowa Basic Skills Tests, report cards, hurdle running speed, Rook, Gin Rummy, board games, and my writing skills.

A World in a Grain of Sand

I recently told my husband, Marlo, my competitive spirit is shrinking. He chuckled.

I have rationalized my minimalist cooking over the years, comforting myself that my cooking minimalism allowed me time to write and to improve my word skills.

Insecure about my cooking, I coped with church suppers by purchasing food: a bakery pie, a Walmart cheesecake, a gallon of soup from a local caterer, or a potato salad from Hy-Vee. I usually disguised the purchases by transferring them to containers from home.

A few weeks ago, for our monthly fellowship supper, my church sponsored its first-ever chili-making contest—with prizes. They asked contestants to write a paragraph about their entry.

A week or so before the chili supper, the chair told me she was concerned. To date, she'd received only one entry.

I had inherited a chili recipe from my mother. I had never made it, but I had loved it as a child. And I had a great story to accompany it. I volunteered.

I immediately wrote the descriptive paragraph: "This recipe has minimal chili, requires minimal preparation time, and has no beans. It is the only version of chili I tasted growing up, the only one my mother made. I didn't know other versions had beans. I didn't know other people called it simply 'chili' until I was an adult and a friend chuckled when she heard me call it 'chili soup.' My first instinct is still to call chili by that two-word name."

Then I dug out my mother's recipe. It called for a can of tomato soup and one of chili beef soup, along with a half-pound of ground beef browned with onions. Hmm. I knew Mother had always used Campbell's canned soups, but I didn't recall seeing a Campbell's chili beef soup on the Hy-Vee shelves in recent years. I checked Hy-Vee; no Campbell's chili beef.

I checked at Walmart; no Campbell's chili beef. I searched fifteen minutes among the hundreds of other soup cans and finally found a "beanless chili with beef" that might suffice. I needed a test run to assure my mother's contest-worthy quality.

It passed the taste test—as delicious as Mom's! I bought supplies for my mother's recipe, times six.

The morning of the chili supper, I browned three pounds of ground beef. My pan was too full; the meat didn't brown. I removed two-thirds and browned it just a pound at a time.

The browned bits stuck stubbornly to the pan. I needed them for flavor! After all, there were prizes involved. I poured in a little water and scraped them loose.

I got the twelve soup cans from the pantry. The Crock-Pot could hold only eight. I added just two pounds of the browned beef and let the Crock-Pot work its magic. After three hours I apprehensively taste-tested this larger batch. Also delicious. Who knows—I might even win!

There were twelve soup entries at that supper, labeled with letters, not names.

Church members tried four-ounce samples. A few tried all twelve options. They voted. The organizers announced the top three soups.

Mine was not a winner.

I was crushed.

"Well, Carol, you don't make chili soup often," Marlo comforted me. "Someone else probably deserved to win."

It was hard to admit he was right.

I rationalized, "My chili soup was very popular. My Crock-Pot was almost empty. Maybe I placed fourth."

Losing the chili contest no longer troubles me.

But one humiliation lingers: Some of those winning cooks' chili stories also surpassed mine.

For my next church supper contribution, I will head to a store.

Section H: Artists and Artisans

45 How Deep Our Need

On our dining room wall hangs a two- by three-foot painting by Elinor Noteboom, junior high art teacher for both my husband Marlo and me. On its left side an Iowa soybean field swirls against the backdrop of a pond, a pasture, and a cloudless sky. On its right side sits a Buddhist garden containing a replica of Mount Fuji, one of Japan's sacred mountains. White, raked stones circle calmly around it, against an unpainted brown foreground and background—Japanese minimalism.

In addition to her roles as wife and mother, Elinor was both a teacher and an artist in her own right—an exception in Orange City, Iowa, in the 1950s. In those years she drew inspiration from Midwestern landscapes, her gardens, and her Dutch heritage.

Elinor and I stayed in touch after I married and moved away from Orange City. When my husband Marlo and I made weekend trips back to Orange City, I sometimes stopped at Elinor's home for coffee and conversation.

In 1984, she toured Japan with other Iowa artists—and was profoundly moved by the tranquility of the Zen gardens of Buddhist monks. Returning to Iowa, she was struck by the similar circular patterns of Iowa's contoured corn and soybean fields. Because of this interest, one year her husband Tom gifted her with a ride in a hot-air balloon, so she could view those contours from above.

Over the next decade she was drawn toward a project which would juxtapose Japanese gardens and Midwestern landscapes. Then her cardiologist informed her that her cardiomyopathy was worsening. "Without a heart transplant, you will likely live just eighteen months," he told her.

Elinor opted out of the transplant list. Seated at her kitchen table, light spilling through the bay window onto her classic face, she said, "I told him to use that heart for someone younger, someone under seventy."

She received new survival orders: a life filled with rest. "That was not easy," Elinor told me. "I had been someone who burned my candle at both ends!" But she heeded his direction, resting whenever she felt the slightest twinge, often for entire days at a time.

Her condition gradually improved, but not before Elinor had learned a lesson in tranquility. And when she began to paint her vision of East meeting West, she launched a sixteen-piece series titled "Prolonged Tranquility," her final major work.

She also defied medical odds, surviving and painting not for just eighteen months, but for ten years.

I was a wife, mother, and business owner juggling multiple roles when Marlo and I attended an exhibit of her Prolonged Tranquility series at Iowa State University in 2004. The peace radiating from the walls in that exhibit was palpable. I wanted to take that feeling home. Since we had missed the exhibit day when Elinor was present, we made a purchase during our next weekend in Orange City.

That painting, the first in Elinor's tranquility series, is now on our dining room wall. Over the years, when I have cradled a cup of coffee in my hands, elbows propped on our oak table, my eyes have followed the painting's gentle curves and paused in its empty spaces. My shoulders loosen, my spine straightens, and my breathing slows.

Over the years, Elinor's painting has been a place to pause, a source of peace.

On the painting, in white ink above Mount Fuji, Elinor wrote these words: "How deep is our need for places of stillness and prolonged tranquility."

How deep indeed.

46 Ceramic Pair

Ceramic busts of an ancient sailor and his wife have stared into the distance from various shelves in my home for half a century, their sagging eyelids covering the tops of their pupils. They have been with me through six moves in three different towns. Boxing them for the moves resulted in black tips on their noses, where a bit of paint rubbed off.

When we were in our twenties, my sister Jan Verdoorn took a ceramics class and made the busts as a gift for me. She used a dry-brushing technique, she told me. She first painted the white bisque black. Then she dipped her paintbrush in a color, brushed most of the paint onto a piece of paper, and dry-brushed the remaining traces of paint onto the pieces, allowing the black undertones of wrinkles in their faces and clothing—and later on the tips of their noses, too.

The woman looks eighty years old. Her husband—I have always thought of him as her husband—actually looks a bit younger, perhaps because a full mustache covers his upper lip and disguises his sunken mouth. Both of their faces are equally wrinkled. I begin to look more like them each passing year, except I cannot imagine my mouth ever being sunken.

For decades, I had thought of them as Russian peasants until a little research on Google Images showed me my mistake. They were cast by Holland Molds in New Jersey, and named "Old Salty Dog" (sailor) and "Old Sea Hag."

Their faces look leathery. The eyes of both, though, are vibrant. I don't know how my sister Jan accomplished that with ceramic figurines and paint. She has always been more coordinated and speedier than I am.

In high school I had a cleaning job for Orange City homemaker Marlys Hassebroek. The job took me three hours each Saturday morning. When I started college, Jan took over. She finished the cleaning in two hours. "I tried to figure out how to make it take longer, but I couldn't," she said. I was jealous.

Her house is artfully arranged with coordinating colors. I have mementos set helter-skelter wherever I can find a surface for them. Her home changes with the seasons. Decorating for Christmas, she creates holiday cheer in every room. I pull out six crèches and a wreath.

When Jan and I play double solitaire, which depends on seeing quickly and placing cards speedily, she whomps me. While I am busy processing a mental sentence about what cards I see, she has already played the next three cards. I process what I see through words; her process is instinctive and instant. I gave up playing double solitaire with her. These days I request we play gin, a slower and more strategic game, where I at least have a reasonable chance of winning.

I have never given Jan a handmade gift because I have rarely done any crafting. The one painting I created when I took an art course hangs in my garage. Even though I painted it as a copy of a print that had hung in my childhood home, the course instructor said it had a poor composition.

I tried crocheting a potholder once using YouTube instructions, and two-thirds of the way through the project, it had turned into a triangle instead of a square,

As we have downsized, I have given away some of my mementos. I consider giving her the busts. I regret I have never given her any handmade craft.

I share this omission with a friend, who reminds me, "Your creativity lies in words. Have you ever crafted words for her?"

Over the next several days, my internal answer to his question is no. Then I remember Jan's eulogies at our parents' funerals. She wrote drafts and requested that I polish the wording. I did. She thanked me. Could I consider those as gifts? I think I could. My regret shrinks.

I decide to keep the busts as a new reminder, not just of my sister and her gifts, but also as a reminder all God's children have different gifts. Someday, I will tell my children that when they dispose of my mementos, they should give the busts to their aunt Jan.

I am now at ease knowing when she receives them she will probably fix those black spots on their noses and find a perfect spot for them in her decor.

47 Enjoying Monet

In junior high, Friday afternoons were special. We had art class! Some days we worked on projects. Other days Mrs. Noteboom pulled down the shades and showed us slides of the paintings by the masters.

One afternoon she showed us Impressionist paintings. I was entranced. I liked their airy quality and the magic of using daubs of paint to create illusions of flowers.

That enchantment stayed with me, so when my husband and I were choosing art for our living room wall, I searched for the Impressionists online. I found a pair of posters that together were a copy of Claude Monet's painting, *The Artist's Flower Garden at Giverny*. Besides being in one of my favorite art styles, the colors matched the pastels of our new couch. I owned a coffee table book featuring Monet's work, but this painting was not on its pages. We ordered the posters and framed them.

Like Monet, I had created my own flower gardens. Monet's painting offered a way to enjoy a garden in my living room, which did not overlook any of my flower beds. His gardens of iris, rose bushes, and trees dwarfed mine. He filled acres; I filled square feet. His gardens boasted vast sweeps of colors; mine had small splashes of them. He paid seven gardeners; I did my own gardening. Like Monet, though, I abhorred bare ground and filled my beds with a profusion of plants.

I enjoyed his gardens, but I didn't covet them. I could enjoy both his gardens and my own. Each had its own inscape, to borrow Gerard Manley Hopkins's term for the unique beauty of each created thing. To paraphrase Hopkins's poem, both gardens were charged with the grandeur of God.

Both Monet and I tried to capture that flaming grandeur, Monet with his paintbrush and I with my 35 mm camera. Neither of us was ever totally satisfied with the results. I took photo after photo of backlit irises, deleted each attempt, and tried again. Monet painted layer after layer, trying to capture his impression of dappled sunlight and light reflections on water. Sometimes he burned multiple paintings, dissatisfied with them.

Monet's paintings were rejected, as were my early writings. I sent off article after article to magazines, whose editors turned them down. Monet was repeatedly rejected by the Paris Salon in an era when photographic clarity and dark colors were in style. In fact, the term "Impressionism" began as a way of mocking the style of Monet and his colleagues.

In 2011 Marlo and I traveled to Kansas City's Nelson-Atkins Museum of Art to view a three-panel display of Monet's huge water lily painting. Each of the panels stood six feet tall and fourteen feet wide. The museum advised visitors to spend time in calm and careful viewing.

So, I did. I sat on one of the benches provided, gazing at the panels which formed an angled grouping in front of me. As my eyes moved over the water and the patches of lilies with no foreground or horizon line, my mind slowed, and I felt a pleasant peace. I was touched later, when I read Monet had said his goal for the painting was to create an "asylum of peaceful meditation in the midst of a flowered aquarium."

We no longer own the pastel couch, and we have downsized to a smaller home. But Monet's painting has gone with us and now hangs in the great room above Marlo's electronic organ. It still fills me with as much pleasure as when I first saw slides of the Impressionists at age thirteen.

I think my art teacher Elinor Noteboom never suspected, back in 1961 in Orange City, Iowa, that her slide show about the Impressionists would still be bringing pleasure to one of her students sixty years later.

Neither did I.

48 Daughter of the Trees

I am a child of the plains. I am a daughter of the trees.

As a daughter of the trees, I have collected art trees for my office wall. *Tree of Life* is a tree cut from tanned leather. The Tree of Life is an archetype in many traditions. As part of the Judeo-Christian tradition, I am reminded Adam and Eve were banned from Eden and from the Tree of Life after they disobeyed God by eating from the Tree of Knowledge of Good and Evil. The leather Tree of Life reminds me of paradise lost.

Oil Drum Tree is cut and hammered from a recycled oil drum. Its birds remind me of the turtledove who cooed from a nest near me when, as a child, I sat in tree branches safely hidden from passers-by.

Tree Holes is a sepia screen print in which the viewer gazes through a giant tree hole at a series of other tree holes.

In childhood, lying in a hammock between two trees, I sometimes wondered about the prairie trees. Did box elder trees produce box elder bugs? Did ash trees have that name because of their gray bark? Why did mulberry trees so often grow in farm fence lines? In that hammock, I met my childhood friends: Beezus, Nancy Drew, the Bobbsey Twins, and the Boxcar Children.

One of those trees also supported a sack swing. Clinging to a rope, the sack swing between my knees, I arced beneath the branches. I thrilled with both weightless excitement and fear.

Creating a leaf collection for a high school biology course, I met trees up close and personal. I learned about deciduous trees that shed their leaves, and evergreens which keep their needles year-round. I learned about simple and compound leaves, about lobed and serrated ones. And I met trees by name: quaking aspen, paper birch, American elm, red maple . . . I learned that vibrant fall colors were present in tree leaves year-round; the colors simply became visible when the green chlorophyll vanished.

Our assigned goal was to collect fifty varieties of leaves and needles. An overachiever, I exceeded the goal and collected seventy, pressing them flat inside the pages of our *Book of Knowledge* encyclopedia set, gluing the leaves to sheets of typing paper, and stacking them in a covered box. A peppery smell wafted from the box each time I opened it. I kept the collection for a decade before I finally parted with it. By that time its leaves were crumbling and colorless.

The trees of the plains are a different breed than the trees of the mountains or the woods. In the mountains the trees grow gnarled and squat, desperately sucking life from the rocks. In the woods they grow straight and narrow, fighting for sunlight by growing leaves only on their topmost branches. On the plains trees often stand alone. Like the prairie trees that surrounded me, I grew up feeling solitary and alone. Books and trees were my best friends.

Seated at my office keyboard, the solitary writer the solitary child became, I gaze again at the trio of artwork on my office wall.

Tree Holes was created by my junior high art teacher Elinor Noteboom, and it was our first purchase of original art, early in our marriage. Elinor introduced me to the Impressionists who remain among my favorite painters. I can still hear her voice describing the work of Monet and Manet. I hear again the pain in her voice as she talked about the loneliness of being a working mother in the decades of stay-at-home moms.

I remember the bustling Phnom Penh market where we purchased *Tree of Life*. We toured Cambodia on a learning trip to see firsthand the work of World Renew, a service organization dedicated to sustainable development in underdeveloped countries. I am reminded that the Tree of Life reappears in the book of Revelation as part of a new paradise.

I look at *Oil Drum Tree* and picture the Haitian artist hammering the oil drum flat and cutting it with a hammer and chisel. I think of The Work of Our Hands, the fair-trade store where I volunteer as part of a network of first-world citizens assisting artisans in the global south with finding markets for their products.

I think again of those solitary trees on the plains. I see the bees that pollinate them, the sun that shines on them, the rain that waters them, and the birds that eat and spread their seeds.

No, the trees of the plains are not alone.

I think of the teachers who shaped me, the Cambodian World Renew staff member to whom I taught English via Zoom, my fellow volunteers at The Work of Our Hands, and the group of four women I've met with weekly for thirty years.

As a daughter of the trees, I am no longer alone. Perhaps I never was.

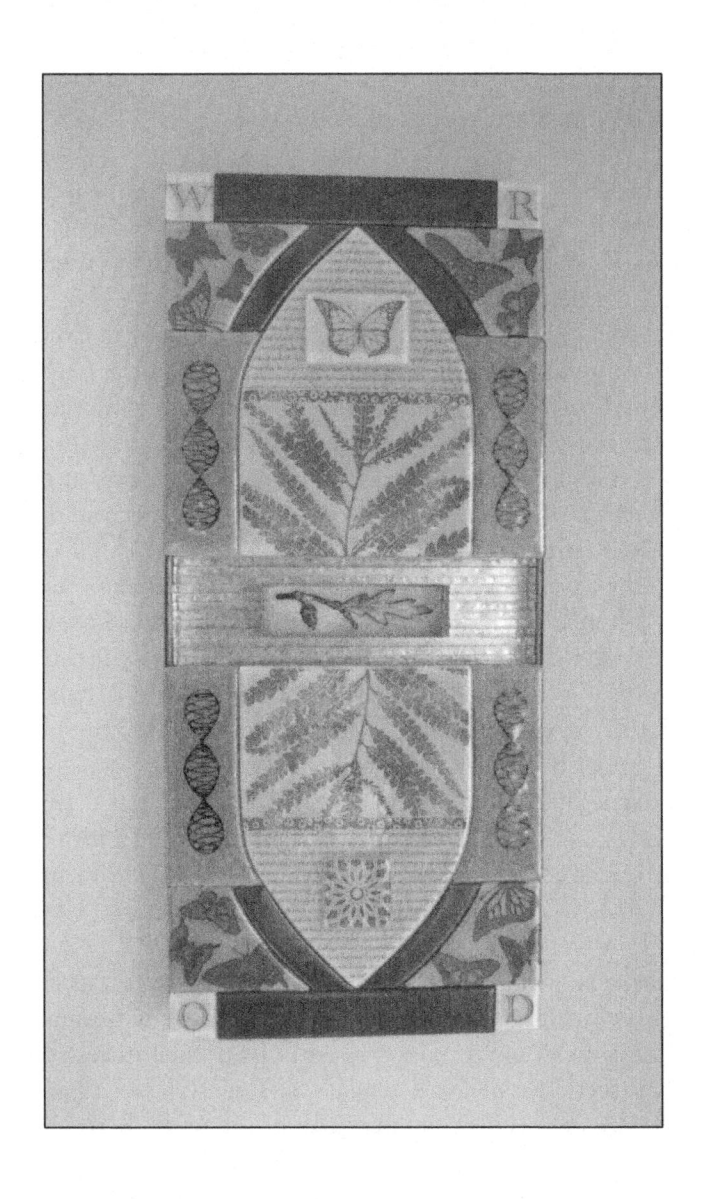

49 Missing Sheryl

Glass artist Sheryl Ellinwood created *Transformation* especially for my dining room after reading some of my writing. "Carol, transformation is important to you," she said, and created a fused glass rectangle with an oak leaf and acorn, butterflies, spirals, and other symbols of transformation, along with some text from Roman Catholic mystic

Thomas Merton. Each corner of *Transformation* has a letter: W, O, R, and D.

As one of my colleagues described Sheryl, "She was a force to be reckoned with."

She was just fifty-five when she died in 2015 from metastatic breast cancer. I miss her.

I first met Sheryl when she chaired the Pella Arts Council. I asked that local council to endorse an application to Iowa Arts Council for funding for *The Dominie's Wife*, a play I co-authored with Mary Meuzelaar. I turned to Sheryl after my request to another organization had stalled due to internal politics and disagreements. With Sheryl at the helm, the process was smooth and seamless. Working together, we discovered we were kindred spirits—both equally right-brained and left-brained. Each of us could be both logical and intuitive, organized and creative.

Sheryl didn't begin her working career as an artist. At seventeen, right out of high school, she began working as a file clerk for Blue Cross Blue Shield, working her way up to account executive, which normally required a BA in marketing. BCBS agreed to give her the position if she would begin work on a marketing degree.

At college, however, Sheryl discovered she enjoyed her elective art classes and dreaded the marketing ones. She reached a turning point. She said, "In one week I went in and I quit my job, I told my husband I wanted a divorce, and I dropped my marketing major. I even switched schools."

She especially enjoyed a glassblowing course. She was crushed when the sculpture professor said he would let her into the program but would never let her use blown glass for any of her sculptures. However, his standard forced her to look at glass differently. "I had to look at the material more metaphorically instead of just, 'Well, here's a blown glass vase, and let's set it on here, and now it's art.'"

She said both blowing glass and using it to create sculptures were creative work, but the sculptures came from a much deeper place within her. When people looked at her sculptures, they were first drawn in by the beauty; then they turned to her and asked a question. It was exactly the response she wanted. "You have to rise above trying to be preachy. I want people to come away with a renewed sense of mystery and questioning."

When Sheryl asked me to help her publish some books in exchange for some of her artwork, I readily agreed. I already enjoyed her blown-glass bowl I had received as a gift.

I enjoy the beauty of Sheryl's blown-glass bowls, vases, and flowers sprinkled around my house, but her sculptures fill me with a sense of mystery and questions. Her three sculptures on our den wall awe me with the reflected light that makes them appear illuminated. She had good reason to name that series *Lumina*.

At my fireplace stands her *Cosmos-Chaos* sculpture, a house atop a circle atop a tall pyramid. It is luminous with red and gold painted metal. Plates of clear glass twinkle with reflected light in silver-blue tones.

Sheryl and I had different roots for our sense of mystery. I was a Protestant Christian in a conservative Calvinist tradition when I began reading Roman Catholic mystics. Sheryl's mysticism began, I think, when she read mystics from Hindu and Buddhist traditions. I embraced the mystics, but I chose to stay within my own Calvinist faith tradition. I think Sheryl chose to leave her faith tradition. But we shared a discomfort with pat answers and preachiness.

I like to think that in the world beyond time we will be able to explore more mysteries together.

50 Scarred Piano

In 1979, Marlo and I bought a dismantled and battered baby grand piano at a bargain price. We had stumbled across it at an inconvenient time while preparing to move halfway across Iowa. We bought it anyway, selling the old upright we already owned and putting the baby grand's parts in our garage.

After our move to Pella, Marlo rebuilt the piano interior. He put in a new pin block and pins, installed new strings, and then tuned those strings multiple times.

I stripped the piano's pockmarked exterior. The delicate grain of African mahogany emerged. I stained the wood, and then coated it with layers of tung oil, which I had learned created a richer sheen than varnish did.

We did not need to replace the ivories on the keys. They had survived the decades unscathed.

After friends helped us transfer the piano from the garage workshop to our living room, I relished the piano's restored beauty. And I loved listening to the music Marlo played.

A World in a Grain of Sand

Except when we traveled, he has played the baby grand nearly every day since. Over the years our rooms have rung with music: classical, sacred, romantic, jazz, show tunes, and more. Each day the beauty of that music has lifted my spirits and filled my heart with joy.

We took good care of our treasure. We did not allow our three sons to use it as a racetrack for their matchbox cars. Neither did they roughhouse anywhere near it. For that, we sent them to the basement.

As the decades passed, though, the finish above the keys began to wear. The stain and tung oil thinned on the vertical wood bordering the keys just below the fall board. Eventually, bare wood appeared in pale semicircles, especially near the two octaves to the left of middle C.

The defects have recently begun to bother me. Today I voice my concern.

"How did that finish get wrecked?" I ask Marlo, pointing to the damage. On the rare occasions I have plunked through a hymn, my fingers haven't come close to the wood.

"My hands are bigger than yours," he says. We match hands. His fingers are an inch and a half longer.

I still don't understand. I curve my shorter fingers against the keys when I play.

"I think it happens when I play octaves," he says. He sits and demonstrates. Sure enough, when he stretches his pinkie and thumb to play two notes an octave apart, his index finger brushes against the vertical wood.

"Octave intervals occur most often in the left hand," he says. Ah, that explains the limited location of the scars that disturb me.

"Perhaps I could use a small cloth and some stain to repair them," I suggest.

"I don't think so," he replies. "That would make it look worse."

He is probably right. Besides, it is more his piano than mine.

But that damage does bother me.

I consider the process of dismantling the piano, stripping that board, and refinishing it totally. That's a major undertaking.

I no longer have the same energy level as forty years ago.

Besides, it might be hard to match the color of the parts I originally stained.

I stare at those flaws. I think, yes, they are scars caused by repeated tiny traumas. But then I realize that trauma was not mine. Minute by minute as the piano finish was traumatized, my soul was bathed in beauty and my heart took flight.

Those scars are not my scars.
I need to make peace with them.
Can I rethink? Can I reframe?
I look at them again. Perhaps I can see them as scallops instead of scars.
Like scallops on a piece of lace.
Like curves on the border of a valance.
It might work.
But it might not.
Well . . . if reframing doesn't work, I shall simply close the piano fall board.
And I shall remember the music . . .
hearing again the rise and fall of the soaring notes . . .
my soul soaring with them.

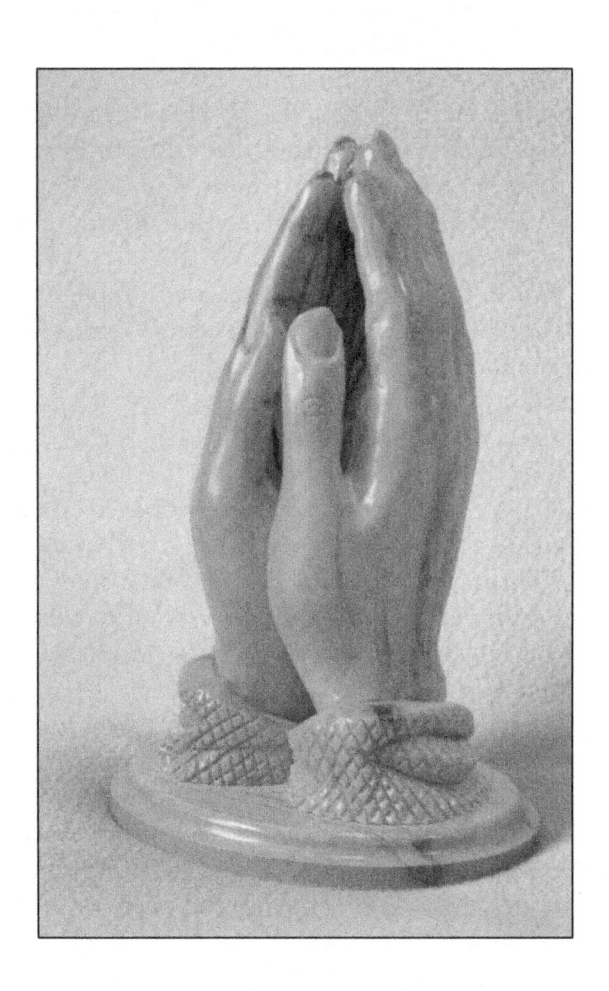

51 Praying Hands

Coming home from a 2008 tour of Israel, Marlo and I each carried with us an olive-wood souvenir. Israeli tourist shops stocked hundreds of olive-wood carvings, many of them religious: rosaries, crosses, crucifixes, Madonnas, Bible covers, Holy Families, crèches, stars, praying hands, and more.

We each selected one olivewood memento to help remember this trip. After all, we had just seen the Mount of Olives where Jesus spent his final night before his crucifixion.

I chose a crèche complete with manger, baby Jesus, Mary, Joseph, a shepherd, sheep, palm tree, and angel. I selected it to join my small collection of crèches. Each Christmas season I unbox them to celebrate the season.

A World in a Grain of Sand

Marlo chose a pair of praying hands. He placed them on his rolltop desk. When we downsized, the hands moved from his desk to a cabinet in our great room where I saw them more often.

Searching for a column topic, I considered my manger scene. *A purchase for a crèche collection? No story there.*

Perhaps Marlo has a story for his praying hands, I thought.

I asked him why he chose them. "I decided a religious carving was a good way to remind me of Israel," he said.

Hmmm. Not much of a story there either.

The hands he bought replicated Albrecht Dürer's best-known pen-and-ink drawing. *Perhaps I can find a story in Dürer's history.*

Wikipedia told me Dürer, a German printmaker and artist (1471-1528), first dyed a paper blue and then used black ink and white highlights for his drawing. He either made it as a study for an altarpiece that was later destroyed in a 1729 fire or made it to carry back with him to Germany when inspired by the virtuoso craftsmanship of Italian Renaissance artists.

I read his brother Albert's hands were his model. I searched more and found a touching story. Albrecht Dürer was one of eighteen children born to a poor German goldsmith in the late fifteenth century. Albrecht and his brother Albert, the two oldest sons, both dreamed of studying at the Nuremberg art academy. They planned to take turns supporting each other through art school. Albrecht won the coin toss. Albert worked in the mines to support him during his art study. When Albrecht finished school, it was Albert's turn.

But Albert said it was too late. Weeping, he showed his brother his hands. Callused, crooked, and arthritic, they had been ruined by his work in the mines.

In tribute and gratitude, Albrecht created a drawing of Albert's hands in prayer. It has become the most famous image in the world of praying hands.

My eyes watered. Then I rejoiced. *What a story! Eureka! I found it.*

I searched for more information. I found additional dramatic detail in multiple versions of the tale. I kept reading.

And then . . .

I found the facts:

Yes, Albrecht was one of eighteen children, but only three lived to adulthood.

Albrecht had no sibling named Albert.

Albrecht's father was comfortably well off, not poor.

A World in a Grain of Sand

There were no mines near Nuremberg during Albrecht's lifetime.

No calluses appear in the drawing, such as would develop during mining work.

The praying hands drawing was created as part of a commission by Jacob Heller for an altarpiece. The same hands appear in several of Albrecht's creations. Art historians believe Albrecht used his own hands for the model.

My eyes widened. *The story is fiction! It is an internet myth.* My shoulders sagged. I sighed.

As I continued to read, I learned the melodramatic tale was copyrighted by J. Greenwald in 1933. (You can read the original version at https://www.learnreligions.com/praying-hands-1725186.) Variations have appeared on multiple websites as object lessons in the value of sacrifice and the need for support from others.

However, the drawing has indeed become famous. It is replicated in many forms, from paintings and plaques to cups and key chains. Justin Bieber even had it tattooed on his leg, just above his ankle. He later added roses.

Well, at least I verified the drawing is famous. But now what do I do?

I tried exploratory writing about hands I remember. I thought of stories about my newborn's tiny fingers, the photo taken of our newlywed hands and wedding rings, and a photo of a child's hand nested inside an ancient one.

I remembered my mother's eczema-scarred palms as she donned rubber gloves to wash dishes, my grandmother's knobby knuckles as she crocheted at lightning speed, and my friend Marilyn's hands, so gnarled she struggled to hold a pencil or a glass of water.

No story arose.

I sighed again. *Perhaps I can't find a tale in these praying hands. Perhaps Marlo's describing them as a way to remind him of Israel is as good as this gets.*

A deadline loomed.

I searched the internet one final time and read Dürer is famous for the quote, "There is beauty in imperfection."

Hmm. His comment is especially true in an era when we all strive for flawless perfection. In life. In art. And even in newspaper columns.

Especially those which fail to find a story.

52 Mysterious Processes

A few grunts escape my mouth as Marlo and I carry the new plant shelving from his garage workshop, squeeze through several doorways, and set it in the sunny window of our den.

Tired, I rest in the glider across from the shelves and consider how to fill them.

A few days later, I select brass planters from a local fair-trade store and purchase two dieffenbachia, two ferns, and a collection of six small succulents. The only remaining decision is what to place in the large hexagon opening at the shelves' center.

A permanent bouquet would be ideal. But I am a flower-arrangement klutz. I usually plop a few fresh peonies in a glass vase, add water, and call it good. For this space, I want something permanent and more beautiful.

A World in a Grain of Sand

I remember my neighbor Janna's wistful look last week when she told me about an unusual dream. She said, "The dream was so detailed and vivid! I jotted some notes about it as soon as I woke. I wish I could write like you do."

"I'd be glad to help you sometime," I offered. I suspected she wouldn't accept my offer.

Today I think, *Perhaps she would be interested in a trade.* I have seen her arrangements, and I know I will be wowed. Janna can create floral masterpieces.

I phone Janna, propose a trade, and she accepts. She asks what I have in mind. For hours, I fumble with ideas. Frustrated, I finally exclaim, "I don't know what I'm doing! If I give you a budget, could you just create something? I am sure it will be beautiful."

She asks questions, suggests a vase from her collection, and works her magic.

A few days later, she delivers an arrangement—ahead of schedule and under budget.

Over coffee, I ask about her process. She mentions mathematically correct height, odd numbers of items, and starting with a line—upright, zigzag, curving, or curled. Then words such as "stability, beauty, conformance, design, expression, drama, emotion, and mood" tumble from her mouth.

My head spins. She sees my befuddlement and leads me to her garage. She shows me the beginnings of an arrangement for a dinner to celebrate a retirement. First, she tells me her limits. She needs something masculine and outdoorsy. Her budget is small. And she wants it to be a memento the retiree can keep.

I see tall cattails and reeds rising gracefully from two artificial logs. She shows me other options she discarded before purchasing the logs. She opens her cupboard doors, revealing shelf upon shelf of containers. She points overhead to the open shelving with dozens of dried flowers from her gardens.

She tells me the arrangement's height is 1.5 times greater than the height of the base. She shows me its curved vertical line.

I ask when she began arranging flowers. She says in 1965 she helped her mother decorate for the Pella Garden Club's Christmas Tour of Homes. Three years later she joined the garden club, showed a few arrangements, and won a blue ribbon. She took flower-arranging classes, and the awards multiplied. Each year, she now submits multiple arrangements to flower shows across Iowa. In June 2024, her Table

Artistry arrangement took Best Overall at the Federated Garden Clubs of Iowa State Show.

Janna's visual creativity began much earlier, however. In childhood she loved draping and shaping crepe paper and fashioning May baskets from construction paper. Art was her favorite class.

I feel a click of recognition. Our differing lives have parallels. Reading, not art, was my favorite subject. In first grade I won a blue ribbon for a poem. I submitted multiple poems the following years.

Words describing writing tumble through my mind. The words "precision, clarity, scene, dialog, suspense, deadwood, variety, lead, and conclusion" are probably as mysterious to Janna as her arrangement vocabulary is to me.

When writing, I also work within limits. "It Has a Story" columns need five hundred to nine hundred words. And, of course, the item I feature must have a story which can gradually unfold for its readers.

I approve the bouquet. Janna's work for me is completed. I ask when she wants me to work on her writing project. "In a couple of months," she says. Her calendar is full until then.

She shows me the notes she wrote on her dream. They include a list of various ways families celebrate Christmas. She would like to create a script for a meeting with each table decorated with a theme from her list. She pictures a lamp turning on at each table when she mentions that Christmas activity.

She has provided my limits: a script for an event with visuals. The event will combine both our skills.

God has wired the two of us differently.

Returning to the den, I study the completed shelving. Then I picture the India copper artisans who hammered, fired, shaped, and polished the copper planters. I remember Marlo drawing blueprints, measuring, sawing, assembling, and painting in his garage workshop. I think of the greenhouse sowers and growers, the truckers, the retail shops.

God has wired everyone differently. It required differing skills and a global village to create this pleasure in my den window. It required the same global village for all the objects whose stories I have shared on these pages, and I am grateful.

And I am thankful for you, dear reader of this book, for letting me share these stories with you.

Best wishes to each of you as you do the shaping and molding you have been created for, including perhaps writing some lively little stories of your own.

More of Carol's writing can be found in her online Substack newsletter *Notes from the Prairie* at:
carolvanklompenburg.substack.com

Group Presentations Available

Carol Van Klompenburg not only writes books; she also offers performances for Iowa churches, social groups, senior centers, clubs, sororities, gardening groups, and more. She has a master's degree in theater arts and has crisscrossed Iowa as part of Firefly Productions, providing readers theater presentations sponsored by Humanities Iowa. She currently offers reading performances, from both her own writing and the writing of others.

Carol custom-creates presentations upon request for entertainment or for education, as desired. Presentation length can range from fifteen minutes to an hour. Available presentations include:

- **Armchair Trips.** Photos and narration for virtual trips. Appropriate for senior groups, especially for those who no longer travel. They last one-half hour. Options include "Blue Danube," "Bridges of Madison County," "Eastern Iowa," and "New England in the Fall."
- **Creative Aging.** Selections from the book by the same title, chosen based on group preferences.
- **Flower Gardening Joys and Trials.** Selections from *Tending Beauty: Forty Moments in My Gardens,* chosen based on group preferences.
- **Growing Up in Small-Town Iowa in the 1960s.** From *Child of the Plains: A Memoir,* selections chosen based on group preferences.
- **A Christmas Collage.** A collection of stories about true Christmas events in the past, both humorous and painful. Especially appropriate for church groups.
- **Christmas Traditions.** A look at Christmas traditions now and in the past. Traditions include stockings, gifts, feasting, cookies, carols, gatherings, trees, cards, and creches. Adaptable for either church groups or other organizations.
- **A World in a Grain of Sand: Lively Little Stories of Household Stuff.** Selections from the book by the same name, chosen based on group preferences.
- **Widows Moving Forward.** Especially appropriate for gatherings of widows and widow support groups.

If you have in mind a topic not listed above, suggest it to Carol, and she will consider creating a new presentation. Carol restricts her engagements to groups in Iowa or in adjacent states and close to the Iowa border. To learn more, email **Carolvk13@gmail.com.**

Audience Praise for Carol's Presentations

Carol tailored her presentation to be of great interest to the audience. Our committee received super-positive feedback from the widows who attended. Even our food servers left awed and greatly encouraged by Carol's words.

Carol was poised. Her vulnerability and insight were outstanding. Her gift with words was exceptional, and she held the women's attention every second.

Norma De Vries
Committee Member, Widows Moving Forward

We invited Carol to speak at a dinner the deacons held for the Seasoned-Singles and Over-Eighty groups from our church. I recommended her to the other deacons after hearing her present at Pella's library. Both times she brought listeners back in time, describing events from our own childhoods.

One story revealed her struggle with making a change in her cell phone as she wrestled with technology. Hers was a struggle all of us older adults have faced as we feel belittled by modern technology but can't live without it.

We concluded with sharing our connections with the stories and our own memories, realizing we are all in this crazy world together!

Marianne Vink
Deacon at Faith Christian Reformed Church

One spring, Carol entertained us at two different Hearthstone Facilities by reading selections from her book *Tending Beauty*. Afterward, several residents told me how well she brought the stories to life as she read them. Many had gardening experience and identified with her experiences. We laughed out loud at her true story "A Chipmunk Saga in Three Acts."

Carol also taught an eight-week workshop on writing your memories to our Independent Living residents.

Connie Boat
Lifestyle Coordinator at Hearthstone,
A Ministry of Wesley Life

When Carol spoke to our church group, she read excerpts from her books, sharing many of her personal experiences. Her reading sparked special thoughts and memories for members of the group. They really could relate to her.

Although sometimes serious, her presentation was also light-hearted and sometimes made us laugh. Many in our Young at Heart Group told me later how much they enjoyed the afternoon.

Christy Van Zee
Leader, Calvary Church Senior Group, Young at Heart

Additional phrases audiences used in response to presentations:
"Gracious"
"Engaging"
"Thoughtfully prepared"
"Professional, qualified, credible"

Other Recent Books by Carol Van Klompenburg
Available from Amazon.com or Carolvk@gmail.com

Creative Aging: 52 Ways to Add Life to Your Years

As you read, you will chuckle and recognize yourself. You will learn how to respond to the passing years and add life to the coming years. When Carol retired, she convinced herself old age was ten years in the future. To prepare for that future, she began researching the topic. She discovered that, like many her age, she was in massive denial. That future was now. She launched a popular newspaper column to share both her life and her learning. *Creative Aging* is a collection of those columns.

Child of the Plains: A Memoir

Growing up in Orange City, Iowa, Carol Van Klompenburg thought the whole world ate Sinterklaas cookies. Descended from sturdy Dutch folk, she is indeed a child of the plains. Carol's childhood memories are both funny and poignant. She guides readers through her parents' World War II romance, her tears in a school principal's office, and her terror that Jesus would return to earth while she watched her first-ever movie. Whether she is reminiscing about her grandparents or revealing her still-active hoarder heritage, readers from small Midwestern towns will identify with her and find themselves reminiscing about their own childhoods.

Available only from Carolvk13@gmail.com

Tending Beauty: Forty Moments in My Gardens

Whether you garden a lot, a little, or not at all, you will relish your forays into the garden alongside Carol Van Klompenburg. Using prose, poetry, and color pictures, she marvels at a butterfly, grumbles at chipmunks, makes war on weeds, and relishes the beauty of flowers. As she plays with words, she sheds light on both the inner and outer worlds of the gardening experience. (50 stories and poems, color photos, $20.00, shipping included.)

Made in the USA
Monee, IL
04 December 2024